BOOKS BY ROBERT NORWOOD

INCREASING CHRISTHOOD

ISSA

HIS GLORIOUS BODY

THE MAN WHO DARED TO BE GOD

THE STEEP ASCENT

THE HERESY OF ANTIOCH

MOTHER AND SON

HIS LADY OF THE SONNETS

THE WITCH OF ENDOR

THE PIPER AND THE REED

THE MODERNISTS

THE MAN OF KERIOTH

BILL BORAM

INCREASING CHRISTHOOD

INCREASING CHRISTHOOD

BY

ROBERT NORWOOD

RECTOR OF ST. BARTHOLOMEW'S CHURCH IN THE
CITY OF NEW YORK

CHARLES SCRIBNER'S SONS

NEW YORK · LONDON

1932

TO
CHARLES VERNON

FOREWORD

This book is naturally an extension of *The Steep Ascent* and of *His Glorious Body*. Their reception has encouraged me to have faith in what so many people have found helpful. It is offered to my friends who have followed me in the noontide meditations at St. Bartholomew's.

It is offered in humility and gratitude: One must be humble in the presence of those mysteries which pertain to the kingdom of God, and one must be grateful for the affirmations of so many friends concerning the validity of the gospel of Christhood which continues more and more to hold and constrain me as I preach.

This series, which represents the meditations of the past two years, was reported stenographically and is offered as they were given at the time of preaching. I have arranged them in chapters.

I acknowledge my debt to Doctor Moffatt's translation of the New Testament and to the publishers, McClelland & Stewart, and Double-

day, Doran & Company, for some lyrics which
I have used in these meditations. I have found
it helpful at times to make my own paraphrase
of the New Testament but I have relied mainly
upon the King James' version and Doctor Moffatt's translation.

Because my themes have selected me, I have
spoken intimately of that which I have found
along the ascending path of Christian discipleship. If the reader is disposed at times to call
me dogmatic, I plead in defence my convictions
which have been shaped through the years and
have so moulded my life that I can only offer
what I have—and with all my might. In fact,
I would not present these meditations in book
form did I not believe that what has meant so
much to me does not belong to me. I must give
of that which I have received. Christianity is a
fellowship in Christ, the proclamation of an inheritance attained; and I should have no right
to a pulpit like St. Bartholomew's if I withheld
what I believe to be the essence of the gospel.

Let me assure my readers that nothing of a
critical nature found in these meditations was
uttered apart from its bearing on myself.

Preaching, as I understand it, is a conference, an Emmaus walk. There is debate and disagreement in such a walk, but out of it comes the sense of One who walks with us even as we argue and, in the end, blesses us with the breaking of the bread and the drinking of the cup of the wine of the new testament. Christianity is a new testament concerning the importance of man, who is no longer under the rule of fear but in the bondage of love. I believe that there would be no further quarrel among the companions of Christ if we accepted the inner testimony of the gospel; that testimony is, as St. Paul said: "The Spirit itself beareth witness with our spirit, that we are the children of God: and if children, then heirs; heirs of God, and joint-heirs with Christ; if so be that we suffer with him, that we may be also glorified together."

I only know that, as I came to understand this inner testimony and accepted it wholeheartedly, life for me began to change. I was no longer in bondage to the old fears. I discovered that I was walking in the newness of life as I found it in Jesus. I salute with reverence all the earlier companions of the path of Christhood.

I do not blame them for what seems to me blurred thinking. The Father's house has many rooms and, as we change from one abode to another, the former things pass away and all things become new.

So this book is offered in humility and in gratitude as of one saying with St. Paul, "I for one do not consider myself to have appropriated this; my one thought is, by forgetting what lies behind me and straining to what lies before me, to press on to the goal for the prize of God's high call in Christ Jesus."

ROBERT NORWOOD.

TEDHOLM,
    HUBBARDS, NOVA SCOTIA,
        September 3, 1932.

ACKNOWLEDGMENT

Grateful acknowledgment is hereby made for permission to quote from the following: *The Piper and the Reed*, by Robert Norwood, copyrighted 1917 by the George H. Doran Co.; *Bill Boram*, by Robert Norwood, copyrighted 1921 by the George H. Doran Co.; *Lanterns in Gethsemane*, by Willard Wattles, copyrighted 1918 by E. P. Dutton & Co.; *His Lady of the Sonnets*, by Robert Norwood, copyrighted by McClelland and Stewart. *Issa*, from which several quotations are taken, was copyrighted in 1931 by Charles Scribner's Sons.

CONTENTS

PART I

INCREASING CHRISTHOOD

PART II

THE MYSTERY OF INCARNATION

[xv]

CONTENTS

PART I

INCREASING CHRISTHOOD

I

THE NEWNESS OF THE SECOND-BORN

WE can meet the challenges of today only by
knowing clearly what are the fundamentals of
our faith in Jesus. We must return to the New
Testament to discover for ourselves these fundamentals as they are recorded. Our age is a conscious age. There have been periods in the history of man when consciousness was heightened
but never more so than in the age to which we
belong, with its inrush of a new science, a new
psychology, and a new theology. These must be
faced by people who are committed to the way
of Jesus.

There is a wide unrest in the world not only
outside the Church but in the Church. We do
not seem to be able to agree about anything,
except this: that Jesus is important beyond any
other experience open to us. I am speaking, of
course, for the Church. Outside the Church it
is denied that Jesus is important. He has never
been more roundly repudiated than he is by

the world of this hour. But the difficulty confronting us is the dispute that is rending the Church asunder, the dispute about the Master.

What has caused the dispute? An old error which was inevitable for many centuries. When I was a boy, I believed that the Gospels of Matthew, Mark, Luke, and John had been written under the immediate direction of the Holy Ghost; that they were inspired verbatim—and consequently what was said could not be questioned; that the ideas which were communicated by these four Gospels were literally true. It had not come to me that behind the four Gospels there was a simple oral teaching which was concerned only with telling what Jesus actually said. It was not concerned with what Jesus did; that came later. But the first disciples of our Master, who began the group to which we today lovingly belong, were interested in the teaching. They regarded that as the gospel.

The gospel was not a story about Jesus. It was Jesus' message. What did Jesus think about life—life that included God and man? What did he think about human conduct? What did he think of the objective of human experience?

Did he throw any light upon the immortality of the soul? Did he prove that the soul is unaffected by death? Did he claim anything for himself that he did not concede to all believers?

These thoughts were uppermost in the minds of the first disciples. They had listened to their Master who had trained them through simply constructed sentences. Whenever we come upon the teaching of Jesus, we are impressed with its simplicity. "The common people heard him gladly." They heard him gladly because they understood him; though he was giving to men the profoundest and most unusual teaching that has ever come from human lips, they understood it.

The mothers, for instance, had no difficulty in understanding what Jesus thought about children. When he said, "Suffer the little children to come unto me, and forbid them not; for of such is the kingdom of God," they knew what we know today—that there had not appeared any man of importance speaking so definitely about little children as this Teacher from Nazareth.

The rest of his teaching was in harmony with

that utter simplicity and tenderness. The disciples knew that Jesus felt tenderly about men and women and children. They knew that the uppermost thought in his mind was the love of God. He believed that what was wrong with the world was that it did not know God as love, and so, whenever he spoke of God, he said, "My Father and your Father." He never claimed the Fatherhood of God in any sense different from that which he taught as our right also to claim. When the disciples asked him for a prayer, he said: When you pray, say *Our* Father. Remember, God is everybody's Father. All men and women and children, whether they know it or not, are children of God. Discipleship begins with the recognition of the truth that God is every man's Father. Our Father . . .

It did not dawn on me in those boyhood days that Jesus never taught anything about himself. I had been reading the four Gospels and believed that the doctrines concerning Jesus found there, stated by those who were recording them, represented the exact nature of what Jesus communicated to his disciples about himself.

One of the arrows which agnosticism and atheism shoot against the Church is the fact that the Gospels, as they are today, were not written by any of the original witnesses. Once we have faced this fact, we discover that many things which are claimed as doctrinally true have no historical basis. If the Church is to go on, this must be accepted. The disruption that is happening in the Church today is due to an intellectual cowardice, the greatest sin of which a body of believers can be guilty. We have had too many doubting Thomases, disciples who are afraid of the facts.

The original gospel was an oral doctrine. It came from the Master himself to his disciples. Some of you may say, "If it is true that the original gospel was oral and not literary; if the Gospels as we have them were not written by any of the original witnesses, how can we know when Jesus speaks?"

Anybody who studies art can distinguish, if he is a real student, an original from an imitation. Any one who is saturated with music knows when Beethoven speaks. Any one who knows the poets needs no codex, no annotations, no footnotes, to tell him who is writing. If you are a lover of Whitman, you will find the good gray poet though his lines be scattered through such a mass of newspapers it may take you a year to read them. And if you know Jesus, if you have come upon certain indubitable historical statements of the Blessed Master, you will recognize all the rest, however they may be scattered through a vast body of doctrines.

Doctor Easton in his splendid book, *Christ in the Gospels,* says definitely and clearly that the Sermon on the Mount represents a collected group of sayings; that there is no historical evidence for a time when Jesus actually gave a sermon of that character. But, however the four Gospels differ in their wording of what Jesus is reputed to have said, they always represent his spirit. An idiom of unusual beauty is manifest whenever an unmistakable saying of Jesus comes straight from his lips. No one can doubt that, before he went away, he said to his disciples, "A new commandment I give unto you, That ye love one another; as I have loved you, that ye also love one another." When John reported him as saying, "God sent not his Son into the world to condemn the world; but that the world through him might be saved," he succeeded in sending through the ages to this hour Jesus' emphatic assertion that he had not come to judge or to find fault with any one. He had not come to announce a God who was a judge. Whoever teaches a day of judgment does not know Jesus. Whoever describes Jesus or God as a judge has never met the Blessed One of Galilee. Jesus' God is no respecter of persons. He is eternal and limitless loving. That love falls on every head and may be appropriated by those who are willing to receive it.

Jesus never exacted any creedal test. He was not interested in philosophies or theories of life. "Master, who did sin, this man, or his parents, that he was born blind?" Jesus answered, "Neither hath this man sinned, nor his parents: but that the works of God should be made manifest in him." Two theories of life were presented. Jesus was interested in neither. He did not deny the theories. But he put the stress on something higher and more important.

The two theories are as rife today as they were then. The world outside—the world of science—teaches that heredity and environment determine personality—personality describing, of course, our physical as well as our psychic properties: we are derivatives from yesterdays.

"Who did sin, this man, or his parents?" Science says, "His parents."

"Who did sin?" An old mystical answer tells us something about karma,—that the embarrassments which we have to face in life are unpaid debts. Though Jesus seems to have accepted that, he did not regard it as important: "Thou shalt by no means come out thence, till thou hast paid the uttermost farthing." We come to the essential thing. Do not think, said Jesus, of heredity or of karma, but think of this: that, after all, through human experience the glory of God is manifested in man. His answer was a refusal to be involved in philosophical speculation and argument. His reply was: Life manifests the glory of God, and when you come into the presence of God, you are released from all debts.

II

God visits mankind by exceptional men and women. When a man is ready for the vision, God grants it. God is always shining forth through the universe, and wherever souls are luminous enough to convey that eternal light, first into their own consciousness, and second out to the consciousness of others, a prophet has happened.

As a little boy Jesus studied the prophets. We know that from one of the first sayings which Luke has recorded: "Wist ye not that I must be about my Father's business?" Early in his youth Jesus made the only discovery worth making on this planet: that God is a Father. He is not an energy. He is not a thought-substance. He is not the sum total of the mass of matter. He is not "a Power not ourselves making for righteousness." He is all that we mean by a person. We drift away from Jesus when we lose the sense of the personality of God.

Many people are disturbed because it is not clear to them just what is meant by the word *personality*. As we ascend in the order of consciousness, we discover that the word *person* increasingly equates consciousness. A genius is a being who has more consciousness than average people, and the scope of that consciousness gives

[11]

to him a sharper picture of the meaning of the word *person*. It gives to those who come in touch with him a sharper picture of what is meant by *personality*. If we go back to the bathybian slime out of which our organisms are said to have arisen, we discover that the nearer we get to that source, the farther away we draw from what we mean by personality; that as we leave that original protoplasm behind and come into the ascending orders of humanity, the word *personality* more and more describes the distance between bathybian slime and the glory of an anointed consciousness.

Jesus began with the conviction that God is One to whom man can speak; that man is derived from God; that somewhere in himself, with all his faults, there is a holy place where God and man meet. When the Jews built a temple, they built it on the plan of what they believed any man to be. The part of the temple that was most sacred was that veiled from the rest of the courts. It was called the Holy of holies. They meant to teach that there is something in every man that is the Holy of holies. That Holy of holies is the soul. You may call it what you like, but we use the word because it has passed into popular understanding and describes what Jesus meant when he said, The kingdom of God is in you. . . . When you pray, enter into that Holy of holies. It is the only place where we can meet God, because it is the only place where God can be in human consciousness. God can only be where He is of nature resident. God is of nature resident somewhere in man. That place Paul described when he spoke of being "strengthened with might by his Spirit in the inner man."

Jesus was a prophet because he made the discovery without which no man can prophesy. Truth does not come from the outer man. It comes from the inner man, and it is only as we have discovered the inner man that we can speak with authority, that we can rule our lives with a manifested power which links us with an increasing Christhood.

From the time that Jesus, as a boy, had made that discovery,—which every one of us must make before we can call ourselves Christians, before we can draw near to Jesus and salute him as Master—until his appearing at the river

Jordan, Jesus believed himself to be a prophet. When we study a prophet, we discover that he has one sign in common with his order—freshness. He may use old words, but how new he makes them! He may outwardly appear like other men, but what a shining quality there is in his personality! How independent of everybody he is, and yet how humble! Jesus is in the order of prophets to the very end, when we see him at the Last Supper, kneeling and washing his disciples' feet, as though to say: You must regard me as a servant. You must look upon me as a bearer of the light, and then you, too, will be bearers of that light which lights every man who comes into the world—the inner man, the divine man, the eternal man, who always was, who is, and who always will be in the being of God.

Attacks are made on Christianity by unbelievers who are opposed to the thing for which Jesus stands, who do not want him. Wherever they find a contradiction in the gospel, they blaze it abroad in the world. Many of our young people have made up their minds that Christianity is a myth, that there is no real history

in it, that it is a beautiful and pious speculation, charactering a group of simple-minded
fishermen of Galilee in the first century; therefore they will not bring themselves under the
law of Jesus. We believe that they would like
to, that there is something in every boy's heart
that is like the heart of Jesus when he said to
his mother, "Wist ye not that I must be about
my Father's business?" We will not believe that
any young woman instinctively wants to deny
Jesus. We believe that many of them are like
Mary crying in the garden, "They have taken
him away, and we do not know where they have
laid him." Because we believe that to be true, we
want to prove that Jesus is real, that the argu-
ments used against him are invalid.

On the other hand, we are conscious of the
fact that in the Church there is still a tragic
stupidity, stubbornness, and persistence, de-
manding of modern men and women a belief in
something the apostles never dreamed of establishing—the inerrant and verbatim infallibility
of the four Gospels.

The important thing for us today is to discover what Jesus really taught, to put the em-

phasis there, to draw from the doctrine of Jesus our own conclusions as to his nature and his place in our spiritual economy. There will always be differences of opinion among the disciples as to the exact nature of Jesus' Christhood. John's deductions concerning the nature of Jesus are altogether different from those of the Synoptic Gospelers. When from the simplicity of Mark we come into the full-orbed rhetorical rush of the Fourth Gospel, we see what a wide divergence there was among the original disciples in their description of the Christhood of Jesus.

Some of them thought of Jesus in terms of the Hebrew Messiah. The Greeks could never understand the Jewish doctrine of the Messiah, but they could understand their own doctrine of Christ. They had been believing in Christ for centuries. They had a picture of Orpheus on a cross. Plato had anticipated the death of Jesus when he described God coming to earth, or, as he would have it, one of the gods, and said that if one of the gods were to come to earth, people would only put him to death. The story of Orpheus is the story, told centuries before Jesus

appeared, of God manifested in a glorious character, and rejected. When we read the great
poem of Æschylus, or when we come to Shelley
with his description of the god who brought fire
down to earth being at last released, we have no
difficulty in seeing that the Christ-concept is as
old as human consciousness. There is something
inherent in consciousness, that demands Christ.
The Christ-idea has been a growing idea from
the beginning. We call Jesus the Christ because,
when we have studied his doctrine and the witness of those who knew him in the days of the
flesh, we regard him as having manifested
Christhood in a way which we do not find any-
where else in the story of exceptional men and
women.

We have seen that the Gospels began with an
oral tradition. Jesus framed his doctrine in simple and unforgettable sentences. His disciples
could never forget these words. So the heart
of the gospel is in this oral teaching, which we
believe, in spite of a few minor changes, comes
down from the lips of One who spoke as never
man spoke, through all the ages of believers, to
us, hearing them with the same joy that trem-

bled upon the lips of Peter when, outside the synagogue of Capernaum, he cried, "Lord, to whom shall we go? thou hast the words of eternal life!"

III

A prophet like Jesus and in the order of his kind is distinguished by the quality of newness. A prophet-mind makes all things new. He does not create them, but he re-issues them. Since there is nothing in the universe but God Himself, there can be no such thing as originality, if by that word we mean a new creation. There is only one new creation—rebirth. As we are born into spiritual reality, we are original. There is no other originality. A prophet is a second-born soul. Jesus was second-born as well as first-born. His words impressed people with their newness.

When he had ended a certain group of sayings, the people were astounded not only at the sayings but at the substance of the sayings. In order to measure the newness of the sayings of Jesus, one needs only to go back to the New Testament itself. The reaction of those in authority to the doctrine that Jesus was giving shows how shocked they were. They could not bring themselves to understand one who appeared as a teacher and yet brushed aside everything they held holy. Jesus did not set aside anything that was holy, but only substitutes for holiness. Man is fond of substitutes, because derivatives are easier to assimilate than originals. It is easy, by memory, to derive an old emotion. Tennyson sang,

". . . a sorrow's crown of sorrow is remembering happier things."

But that does not go deeply into the facts. There is no sorrow like its first impact, no joy equal to that moment when it is suddenly born. We fail life because we are too lazy or too occupied to recapture our first emotions, whether of joy or of sorrow. It calls for hardihood of the spirit to be constantly in a state of renewal, to be steadfast to ultimate things, to be determined never to accept their substitutes. That is the reason why we so frequently fail in our friendships. We have lost the first rapture and to regain it calls for a fine discipline of our relations. It is because we lower those relations that we lose the original ecstasy out of which they sprang.

This is an outline of that quality in Jesus which from the beginning set him and still sets him apart from all other teachers. There was a newness not only in his voice but in the teaching itself. And it demanded an entire change of thought.

In the New Testament repentance does not mean giving up one kind of emotion for another, but forsaking one mode of thinking for another. Repentance means change of thinking. It is a mental experience. We cannot have a devotional life apart from an intellectual integrity. An emotion that springs from subsidiary facts is perilous as well as unreliable. It is only as we strive to bring our thinking up to the highest that we can be certain of our emotions.

"The people were astonished at his doctrine." From the beginning, religious people had invariably thought of God as apart from man. God lived in the heavens. It was part of their crude cosmogony to situate God above the sun and the moon and the stars and the planets.

If one wanted to reach God—so thought the psalmist—one had to climb up into the heavens, or go down below the foundations of the earth, or take the wings of the morning and dwell in the uttermost parts of the sea. Better that concept of God than none at all! But it was not what Jesus taught. Therein lies the newness of his doctrine. You do not need, he said, to take the wings of the morning and fly to the uttermost parts of the sea, or scale the skies, or plunge into the nethermost abyss. All you need to do is to draw into yourself. Find yourself!

There was nothing original in the statement, *Find yourself*. Over the portals of the temple at Delphi the same thought was written: "Know thyself." It was the burden of Socrates' teaching. Plato inscribed it on every page of his remarkable books. Yet it sounds entirely new when it comes through Jesus, and that is the quality which sets him apart from men. When his enemies say that he never originated anything, arguing that whatever was taught by Jesus had been taught before, we answer: That does not affect the fact of Jesus and his claim over our lives. Jesus' body was derived from the dust of the ground, as our bodies are derived. His inner man came from God, as we also, in our Christness, come from God. In that Christness Jesus posited his doctrine concerning God and His kingdom.

We have grown so accustomed to Jesus' way of looking at things that it is not easy for us to retake the first impression he created by his teaching. For eighteen hundred years, we have been familiar with the parables, with the Sermon on the Mount, and with the general outline of his character as it is communicated through the New Testament. If we could forget all that and see Jesus as men and women first saw him we, too, should be astonished at his doctrine.

We are familiar with the scribal method, which seeks to establish truth by texts. We meet it continually, not only in the New Testament but everywhere in the world today.

> I know not any fear of thrones,
> No claim of Scribe and Pharisee;
> My word is set to many tones
> Of lute and harp and psaltery.
>
> I have no temple and no creed,
> I celebrate no mystic rite;

> The human heart is all I need,
> Wherein I worship day and night:
>
> The human heart is all I need,
> For I have found God ever there—
> Love is the one sufficient creed,
> And comradeship the purest prayer.
>
> I bow not down to any book,
> No written page holds me in awe;
> For when on one friend's face I look
> I read the Prophets and the Law !*

That describes what Jesus was and what he taught. When the scribes tried to entangle him with their texts, Jesus brushed them aside. He brought men and women directly to life. He would say: Consider life. Let life teach you. Enrich your experience with this planet, and you will find everywhere the oracles of God. Consider the lilies of the field. We have never heard, nor shall we hear, a scribe talk that way. A scribe will thumb his books of texts. If he can find a quotation from some hallowed book, he will quote it. Remember how Burns put it:

> "Ev'n ministers they hae been kenn'd,
> In holy rapture,
> A rousing whid [lie] at times to vend,
> And nail't wi' Scripture."

*The Piper and the Reed, George H. Doran Co.

[23]

Jesus was aloof from all that. We must get back to him as he was in the days of his flesh. Jesus always stands out—wind-blown, sun-tanned, vigorous and strong, with a voice that rolled and carried its music over and over again into the souls of those who, having heard him, could never forget the sound of his voice and the newness of his words.

But our age is not so much the age of the scribe and the Pharisee as it is the age of Nicodemus. To those who ask, "Why do you so frequently strike at the intellectuals?" my answer is: If Jesus were here, he would not say much about the scribes and Pharisees, but he would denounce the intellectuals who sneeringly rule out imagination and emotion, whose whole system of education is to teach young people to be afraid of their emotions.

In one of the pictures we have of Jesus, we find him enjoying the children at play. What history there is behind his words, "The men of this generation are like children in the marketplace." He did not despise the children, but he was amused at the petulance of children who, when they are performing, expect that others will share their deep sense of the reality of what they are trying to communicate: We have piped unto you and you have not danced; you cannot share our laughter with us. Or we have staged a funeral and we have shed real tears, and you have looked at us curiously. There is something in such words deeper than we find when we listen to them. Our protest is against the incurious people who are unaffected by life, who are so hardened by their self-consciousness that they have lost all their enthusiasms. If we were to come into Jesus' presence, he would make us ashamed of our mental hardness.

Nicodemus did not dare to come to Jesus by day; that would have thrown him out of his intellectual caste. He was interested in Jesus; he was disturbed by him. The multiplicity of books being written today by intellectuals like Nicodemus proves that the intellectual is disturbed by Jesus. He cannot get past him. Jesus always will be a challenge to the intellectually self-sufficient. Nicodemus began with his cut-and-dried questions. But he was aware of the fact that Jesus had a relationship with life which his learning had not given to him. He wanted the secret, and Jesus answered definitely: Nicodemus, you must change your thinking. You are thinking too logically. You think you can reduce this patternless plan of existence into patterns. You cannot. Life does not turn upon definitions. The wind blows where it wills. You can feel it but you cannot describe it. But it is blowing upon your face, and everybody who is second-born is conscious of a new ecstasy, of a limitless power, and is released.

Jesus believed his teaching to be important. He sent his disciples out to teach and to preach. One would be beyond humanity if he successfully resisted the temptation of the moment to indicate how untrue to the method of Jesus is the notion that he was interested in anything like an ecclesiastical hierarchy. He was not. Doctor Easton points out in his book that, in the sayings and parables, we find nothing that teaches a sacramental system. That does not mean that we repudiate sacraments. We would take as an illustration Jesus' attitude to the sacrament which John thought important. When Jesus went down to the river, John is reported to have said, "I have need to be baptized of thee, and comest thou to me?" Jesus answered, It is good always to be identified with righteousness. Whatever means much to people, whatever is helpful, we will not destroy it, but we do not base the kingdom of God upon it.

The Church must always remember that a disciple is commissioned either to teach or to preach. Each one of us is bound to go forth now and show, by the way we live, if by nothing else, that we have found and that we are following the way, the truth, and the life. Christianity comes down the ages, through disciples who believed that they had been accepted by the Master because they themselves endorsed the Master's view of life. A disciple is anybody who endorses and follows Jesus' way of living. Baptism, Confirmation, Ordination, have little to do with that discipleship. Our discipleship is based upon the new commandment. We are disciples of Jesus as we have learned the limitlessness of loving. As we are kindly, we are disciples.

My complaint with people is that we are too scornful, too critical, too clever, too analytical, too gossipy. We have missed the great-heartedness of Jesus; and until we have recaptured that

[27]

great-heartedness, we shall come under the rebuke of his blessed words: "Not every one that
saith unto me, Lord, Lord, shall enter into the
kingdom of heaven; but he that doeth the will
of my Father which is in heaven."

We stand in amazement before the simplicity
of Jesus' teaching, its challenge to continue in
simplicity, to believe that we insult life when
we try to imitate any personality other than
that with which we have come into the world,
that the real power in any man's life is to continue himself at his best unto the end.

Make no apologies before your world, even
if you have to stand alone. Be consecrated to
the highest high, as Jesus was, and then there
will be astonishment from the world that meets
you, setting you apart as the possessor of newness—the newness of the second-born, the power
of the re-consecrated.

II

THE GOSPEL OF JESUS

THE Master used two methods of teaching—the sayings and the parables. The sayings were given to the disciples, the parables to people, for he drew a distinction between disciples and people. *Disciples* described those who had come out of the multitude, stirred by the parables, affected by a holy presence, and hungering and thirsting for the deeper mysteries which they knew were in his heart.

The parables, on the other hand, were his salutes to the crowd. He knew that in the crowd were disciples in the making; so he adjusted his teaching to their understanding. That must always be borne in mind when we hear him in a parable. There must have been many more, but the parables that are recorded bear witness to the fact that the disciples themselves were impressed by these utterances and, after Jesus had gone away, they repeated them in their rôle as teachers and preachers.

Whatever we may think of the ministry,

Jesus regarded his disciples as teachers and preachers. He impressed them with his secret and, when they had received it, he said to them, "Freely ye have received, freely give." The things which he regarded as important were committed to them in short and easily remembered sentences, which we find all through the four Gospels. We also come upon them in some of the Epistles, revealing that, after Jesus had gone away, disciples were eager to communicate to the multitudes Jesus' doctrine about life.

So we repeat that the gospel *of* Jesus is more important than the gospel *about* Jesus. We must put first things first, in his spirit who said, "Seek ye first the kingdom of God, and his righteousness; and all these things shall be added unto you." As we read the sayings of Jesus scattered through the four Gospels and some of the Epistles, we discover what he meant by the kingdom of God: consciousness in the human soul of its relationship with God—God as Father and man as son.

The life of Jesus was that doctrine in action. When the disciples began to gather their materials for literary purposes, they communicated the teaching, first, in the sayings, second, in the parables for the multitude, and then in the collection of their memories about Jesus. When we read the four Gospels, we are impressed with the fact that there is never any disagreement among them in reporting the sayings of Jesus. There is little divergence in form when the parables are reported; but there is a wide divergence in form and in substance when the disciples are drawing upon their memories to describe Jesus in the days of his flesh.

According to Doctor Easton, by the year 40 —that is, within ten years of the death of Jesus—there was a fixed oral tradition which included the sayings and the parables. Disciples gathered at Jerusalem were eager to learn more of what the Master had taught, and Doctor Easton has happily described the situation in Jerusalem as fitting into what we might call a teachers' training institute. Within ten years after the death of Jesus, there was in existence a school that had for its purpose the communication of the doctrine of Jesus, which the disciples regarded as more important than their stories about Jesus.

The trouble with Christianity today—and it has been the trouble with Christianity through the centuries—is in the obvious fact that the stories about Jesus have been raised to the same authority and importance as the doctrine of Jesus. Christianity is never divided about the doctrine of Jesus. We all believe that Jesus taught that the true kingdom of God is in the awakened consciousness of the disciple. But when it comes to our attitude toward Jesus, as to who he was, how he came, what he did while he was here, and what happened after he went away, we find ourselves launched into debates and controversies, disagreements and prejudices, dislikes and the sunderings of sectarianism. One day the Church will awake to that fact. When it does, there will be no problem of church union. There is only one basis for the union of believers—accepting what Jesus taught about man, and practising the doctrine. Wherever men have received that doctrine, they have been changed.

I have described second-born men. We know, when we hear the Master speaking as he spoke to Nicodemus, that he believed in this second birth—the new consciousness. Paul described it as a new creation. We have seen that repentance has nothing to do with emotions. Repentance is the ascent of consciousness to a higher and more inclusive plane. When we have attained that new consciousness, all things are become new. We are no longer dominated by the lower consciousness.

St. Paul has made clear what that lower consciousness is. The natural man—man in his bodily or animal or physical states—does not understand the things of God; but when a man has entered into his closet—his soul—and has for the moment ruled out the animal senses, he begins to see himself in a new relationship with God. Then he has a resurrection. He begins the manifestation of his power, bearing about in his physical states the stamp of the spiritual states.

We shrink from accepting this because it means a crucifixion of the former man. We will no longer yield to him. The former man deceives us. He is of the earth earthy. He is related to the animal kingdom. But the second man is the lord from heaven. The lord from heaven is the

inner man which inhabits every body. It is the
discovery of this lord from heaven as identical
with us that leads to victory—the victory which
St. John had in mind when he wrote: "This is
the victory that overcometh the world, even our
faith." Our faith in what? Our faith in ourselves as sons of the living God; our faith in
power to look upon life as Jesus looked upon
life, to be related to that life as Jesus was related, to manifest divine sonship as Jesus manifested it.

When Jesus was asked by his disciples how
to attain this power, he led them to the new
commandment. He did not lean back upon the
Mosaic decalogue. There was no prohibition in
the mind of Jesus. Something is wrong with our
world. The reason why the Church is failing is
because it is linked to the fallacies of the lower
man. The gulf between Moses and Christ is the
difference between prohibitions and affirmations. Jesus affirmed realities. He dealt in positives. Moses was concerned only with negatives.
The decalogue is not a Christian ordinance. It
is not Christian to lean back upon denials. Put
positives in their place, and you shall be

changed—and, in time, shall have part in changing the world.

It is not easy to follow the new commandment. How can one be a lover unless he affirms his Christhood? How can we follow Jesus if we separate his Christhood from our Christhood? May I quote a short poem of Willard Wattles, which seems to me to gather up exactly what Jesus wanted us to learn:

"Says the Christ in me to the Christ in you,
'How do you do, brother, how do you do?'
Says the Christ in you to the Christ in me,
'What do you see, brother, what do you see?'

And the Christ in me bends down an ear,
And answers, 'I hear, brother, I hear;
I knew you once in the long ago,'
And the two Christs answer, 'Yes, I know.'"*

No one can follow the new commandment unless he has accepted the doctrine of Jesus. If you say, "I cannot love the way Jesus loved," I answer: Until your Christhood is identified with his Christhood, you will be a failure. But the moment you enter into the Christ consciousness, love will be as natural to you as breathing. It will no longer be possible for you to enter-

*Lanterns in Gethsemane, E. P. Dutton & Co.

tain suspicions and angers, jealousies and ri-
valries. The authority is a well-known fragment
from Paul's Epistle to the Galatians, contain-
ing almost the entire doctrine of Jesus:

"Brethren, if a man be overtaken in a fault, ye
which are spiritual,"

(and when he says *spiritual* he means *Christed*,
converted from the animal to the spiritual man,
changed from the first to the second Adam)

"restore such an one in the spirit of meekness; considering thyself, lest thou also be tempted.

"Bear ye one another's burdens, and so fulfil the
law of Christ. . . .

"And let us not be weary in well doing: for in due
season we shall reap, if we faint not."

It is remarkable that Paul who did not know
Jesus, so far as we are aware, in the days of
his flesh; who certainly was not trained by Jesus
as his brother disciples were trained, was able to
include in his Epistles the doctrine of Jesus.
This bears upon the statement made by Doctor
Easton that, by the year 40, there was a definite school of teaching, which was concerned
only with what Jesus taught through the sayings and through the parables.

We must not faint in carrying through the entire doctrine of Jesus. The quarrel we have with many people who like to think of Jesus as their Lord and Master, and themselves as his disciples, is that they do not realize that discipleship means candidating for Christhood. We are disciples because we will never be satisfied until we are all that Christ was—all that Christ is. We have no salvation apart from Christ. We want no life here or after death that does not bear the signature of Jesus. And if we want that life after death, we must begin to practise it now. It is important that we should be converted to the life of Christ now; that we should regard as sin whatever interferes with our Christness. And the only way to overcome the interferences with our Christness is to be utterly committed to the law of love.

The one dreadful sin, therefore, against which we must be always on our guard is the sin of negativing our lovingness. Watch carefully, in season and out of season, your thoughts, your words, your deeds—and even more, your moods. Cast out from your consciousness whatever throws shadow upon this planet, whatever darkens the glory of your universe. Why is not the Church preaching that today? Why is it lost in its negations and prohibitions, when the singing clarity of the affirmations of Jesus is written upon our awakening consciousness?

The glorious thing about discipleship is bearing one another's burdens, being gentle with one another, because we are in the group of disciples. If we need at times help and guidance, it is wise to read another portion of this Epistle to the Galatians. How eager Paul is to communicate this doctrine to the group he is addressing!

"By love serve one another.

"For all the law is fulfilled in one word, even in this: Thou shalt love thy neighbour as thyself.

"But if ye bite and devour one another, take heed that ye be not consumed one of another.

"This I say then, Walk in the Spirit."

By the Spirit, Paul meant our Christhood. That same thought links together the stories told in the New Testament concerning the Master himself. In his Epistle, Peter is represented as saying that Jesus was an example, that we might follow in his steps. Jesus demonstrated to man on this planet the life which he must live if he would enter into the kingdom of God.

"Walk in the Spirit, and ye shall not fulfil the lust of the flesh."

When Paul said "lust of the flesh," he meant something more than intemperance in meat and drink, something more than lasciviousness. He was not only touching upon social vice, he was going still deeper. The lusts which Paul regarded with abhorrence are found in their sequential categories:

"Adultery, fornication, uncleanness, lasciviousness,
"Idolatry, witchcraft, hatred, variance, emulations, wrath, strife, seditions, heresies,
"Envyings, murders, drunkenness, revellings, and such like: of the which I tell you before, as I have also told you in time past, that they which do such things shall not inherit the kingdom of God."

Why is it that preachers of today stress certain irregularities of humanity—as though they were the only irregularities! Why should we be fighting against the racketeers, for instance, when racketeering is going on in the group of disciples? Why should we be so ardent against sexual vice, when hating is worse than sexual vice? Our arrogance, our intolerance, are greater sins. Every man knows that when he stoops to physical excesses he is robbing himself of his glory, but he does not know that he is robbing himself of a still greater glory when he submits to hatred, variance, emulations, wrath, strife, seditions, heresies.

The result of being second-born will be manifested in proportion as we manifest these definite reactions of the new life:

"The fruit of the Spirit is love, joy, peace, long-suffering, gentleness, goodness, faith,

"Meekness, temperance: against such there is no law.

"And they that are Christ's have crucified the flesh with the affections and lusts.

"If we live in the Spirit, let us also walk in the Spirit."

The task before us at this hour is to act in obedience to him who said: If you are risen into Christhood, seek those things where Christ is. He sits where God is. He represents to us what our Father is like. Climb, and still climb, until you are one with him in the Father.

II

There are sayings in the New Testament which trace the origin of unbelief in that day to conditions similar to the conditions present in our day. There is a saying ascribed to Jesus: "For the hardness of your heart he wrote you this precept." Then there is Paul's confession, "I verily thought with myself, that I ought to do many things contrary to the name of Jesus of Nazareth," attributing his hardness to the tendency of the natural man to resist the supremacy of the spiritual man.

We admit that, in a world like ours, if one wants to be comfortable, it is best to leave Jesus alone, to have nothing to do with him. We heard of a splendid young man, teaching a group of agnostics and atheists about Jesus. He himself had been an atheist, yet one of the most spiritual young men we know. This is what he said to his group: "Leave Jesus alone, because, if he gets hold of you, you are done for. You will never be satisfied with life as you have been living it. A long, hard road of struggle and anguish is before you. Best leave him alone."

That is the reason why many people substitute Churchianity for Christianity. There is more atheism and unbelief inside the Church than there is outside it if by atheism and unbelief we mean a denial of the life and teaching of Jesus. Every time we hate, we deny the life and teaching of Jesus. Every time we gossip and are guilty of backbiting and slander, we deny the gospel of Jesus. We need only go through the churches of any community, at random, to discover that real Christian discipleship is rare. It is easier to be ritually or morally correct than to be right with the loving heart of Jesus, who said to the correct in his day, "The publicans and sinners go into the kingdom of God before you." Why? Because the way to the kingdom of heaven is through the narrow gate of the human heart. It is determined entirely by the width of our love. Before we can enter into the kingdom of heaven, we must humbly confess that our love is a limited thing. Until we face that, we can never know Jesus or come into the power of his life.

The world still refuses Jesus because it is too lazy, too cowardly, or too physical, to accept him. We are still saying to him as a disciple said after the Resurrection, "Wilt thou at this time restore again the kingdom to Israel?" rather than putting into action the qualities Paul described in the thirteenth chapter of the Epistle to the Corinthians, the preface of which was: "I show unto you a more excellent way." Then he began to tell about love that seeks not its own, that bears all things, believes all things, and continues patient and understanding to the very end.

No one of us can call himself a disciple of Jesus until he has been overwhelmed by the love of Jesus. It was that blinding light which threw Paul down before he reached the gate of Damascus. Suddenly it dawned on him that no religion can be right if there is hate in it. When he measured the hate which he held in his heart against other people's religions and creeds, he came face to face with the sternness of Christ who, from the height of his limitless love, called and said, "It is hard for thee to kick against the pricks." There is a wounding quality in the love of Christ that is the most bitter experience which any soul can endure. Until we have been thrown down, blinded, and even killed by the love of Christ, we shall never know his kingdom; we shall continue as we have been doing through all these years—and as we are doing now—in accepting Christ-substitutes for Christ-realities.

As I listen to conversation at luncheons and dinners, I discover that there is more un-Christ-like hardness among women disciples than among men disciples. Women have more time on their hands, and they waste much of it twittering and talking about unimportant matters. The Church is largely made up of women, and if the Church is to be saved, the women must be regenerated. They must stop their hardness, their gossip, their little-mindedness, their bitterness. They must be humble before the feet of Jesus. They are too sure of themselves. They think that, because no one has ever uttered a word against their character, they are at the very feet of Jesus. They are not if there is bitterness and unkindness and hardness in their Christianity.

Yet there have been no believers from the beginning of Christianity down to the present who have had more power for Christ in their hearts than women. The gospel entered Europe by way of a woman. It was Lydia who estab-

lished, through Paul, the first Church in Europe.
It was through her hospitality that Paul was
able to gain a hearing in a city which at first rejected him. There was never a more unfair story
than the one which represents Paul as being a
man who disliked women. His letters abound in
tender appreciation of his women friends. When
women are really at their best with Christ, they
become his highest emissaries. But they must be
released from little things. The women in our
churches today must turn from their Churchianity. They must stop worshipping leaders, and
worship only one leader, Jesus. They must be
emancipated and must stand forth in the glory
of their own rightness.

All the world knows that, wherever the human
heart is constrained by the heart of Christ, there
is the kingdom and there is the priesthood. As
we turn over the pages of history, we realize that
any theory of the priesthood that makes it a
mechanism is untrue to the facts of the gospel
story. If we are to believe the story, we discover
that the first gospel sermon based on the Resurrection was preached by a woman. One of the
most popular and appealing of the Resurrection

stories is that Jesus revealed himself in his glory to a woman who, before he had transformed her, was so bad that she was full of "devils."

Two great moments in Christianity have to do with a man and a woman—the man was so bad that he persecuted even children and put them and their mothers and fathers to death. That was Paul. And the other was a woman of such notorious character that her history was written in a sentence: "Out of whom he had cast seven devils." It was to her that Jesus appeared and announced himself as the resurrection and the life, proving that, as our love is resurrected to the heights of the love of Jesus, we have power to do wonderful works in his name.

Christianity is a life, not a creed. If every one would admit that, how simplified the whole matter of our religious life today would become! How wrong are they who keep insisting that it is a creed. How wrong are we—how hard-hearted, how obdurate, and how unready to be released to the lovingness of Christ—when we keep insisting that it is still a matter of creed, though the Lord himself has said, "It is not every one who says, Lord, Lord, shall enter into my kingdom." Jesus lived a life. He demonstrated by his life that man is God's son; that, as God's son, man is armed with power against the gates of death and hell; that, when man comes into the consciousness of this divine sonship, the prophecy will be fulfilled that one day the world shall be full of the knowledge of the Lord as the waters cover the sea. He gave his doctrine in his life as well as in his words; and when his life was ended, before he met the cross, he rounded his doctrine with the new commandment, "That ye love one another."

The world needs that witness and that gospel, and it can only receive them as of old it received them—through converted men and women. It is our business to be converted to that truth, to begin with the resolution which Paul made when he said, "God forbid that I should glory, save in the cross of our Lord Jesus Christ, by whom the world is crucified unto me, and I unto the world." By "the cross of Christ" he meant the acceptance of the discipline necessary to receiving the power. We who have passed through the experience know that Jesus' cross was not any harder for him than our cross is for us;

that the hardest of all crucifixions is to nail our hates upon the cross of love.

III

We find in the New Testament moments that are the measurement of the creative urge of men overwhelmed by a mystical experience. Into those moments they poured such ecstasy as we know only when we feel and see something beyond our power to express.

We wish it were possible in this age to preach without being held by the necessity of argument. On the other hand, when we read through the New Testament, we discover that the best things came by way of argument; that there has never been a time in the history of the Church when disciples found preaching easy, because preaching is the effort of confirmed mystics to make mystics out of their audience. Unless one has that sense of the invisible and its reality, one cannot preach. By the fact that his audience is largely unconvinced, the mystic must bring his ecstasy down to meet the conditions which are created by unbelief.

Whatever we may hold about the priesthood,

it does not seem to have entered into the plan of Jesus. He did not organize a priestly ministry. He did not organize sacraments. His scheme of salvation had nothing to do with a hierarchy or a church. These things came later because they had to come. They came because this is a world of organization, and civilization bears witness to the fact that we can do nothing with ecstasies unless we organize them. The ecstasy of music and its companion arts, the ecstasy of philosophy and its companion arts, must all be organized. But that does not mean that the ecstasy itself postulates any specific organization. Jesus brought an ecstasy about God into the world, leaving it to his disciples to organize.

If Rome would accept that, Protestantism and Catholicism would work happily together. The Quaker on the one side and the Catholic on the other, with the Modernist or the Liberal between, would find it easy to go on all the roads of the companionship of Christ. But unfortunately Rome on the one side is convinced of the sanctity of a priesthood including the sacramental system as postulated by Jesus himself. Protestantism on the other side is equally convinced that Jesus relied altogether upon the infallibility of the documents which were written under the influence of his holy spirit after he had gone away. During the Reformation the Protestants formed a slogan, "The Bible and the Bible only." We cannot build Christianity on that. Luther and the Protestant movement rebelled against the unhistoricity of the sacerdotal system with its attendant magical rites of sacraments. Both were wrong. Only St. Paul seems to have caught it, but Luther had a dim vision of it when he developed his doctrine of justification by faith.

Though the controversy is still raging, we are beginning to realize that the one doctrine fundamental to all believers is faith in the supremacy of Jesus. The moment we believe that, we are free to all other opinions and conclusions as well as practices. It is the conviction of many that we are rapidly working toward that in our day. The Roman Church will always be the Roman Church; the Salvation Army will always be the Salvation Army, because we differ as to personality and temperament. But the hard dogma will ultimately go, and there will be left only the great Pauline doctrine of the soul's justification through surrender to the leadership of Jesus.

The original disciples did not have any particular doctrine even about Jesus. They recognized the fact that he was different, because of the beauty of his character, his power, and the searching quality of his words. When a man appears in the world, whose very personality makes people feel ashamed of themselves and at the same time fills them with longing to be better, we must use the word that tradition supplies, until we find a better word to describe him.

There were two words in Jesus' day. The Hebrews said *Messiah* and the Greeks said *Christ*. Both Messiah and Christ meant a man unusually endowed with divine consciousness. When we say *Christ*, when we use the general title *Increasing Christhood*, we stand face to face with an intimacy with God which belongs to every believer who has found it, first of all, historically established in the man Jesus. What better description of Christ do we want than that?

Christianity has to do with only one thing— the demonstration of our indwelling Christhood.

Until Jesus is revealed, not to us, but in us; until we are demonstrating our Christhood because we have met the Christ Jesus, our discipleship is a name only. We cannot prove from the New Testament whether Jesus was virgin-born or not. The documents are too uncertain. We must realize that no doctrine about Jesus over which we quarrel is important, because those doctrines can be either accepted or rejected on the basis of texts, and so that witness is of little value.

The thing that is of value is the witness of Christ in us today. Is Christ in believers? Is Christ working in civilization? Is Christ being manifested through the churches? Is the world becoming more and more aware of the rich inheritance of its divine sonship? These thoughts are occupying the minds of serious people in this hour, and, as the centuries pass, they will come at last to occupy the mind of the Church. If you are debating about miracles and the supernatural, or some theory of church government, you are burdening yourself and making it impossible for your spirit to be released to the redemptive power of Jesus.

We have seen that there is a difference between a gospel about Jesus and the gospel which Jesus himself taught. We must want his teaching, his gospel. We must want to know what Jesus knows about God and about man. And, above all, we must want to know what Jesus thinks about us. Where do we stand in relationship to him and God? Is it possible for us to get rid of the hampering sins that wound our souls? Hear Paul cry, "O wretched man that I am! who shall deliver me from the body of this death?" Who will set me free from the corrupting tendencies of ignoble things? Who will make it possible for me to imitate the Master? Who will make it possible for me to do many mighty works in his name—to heal the sick, to give sight and hearing and speech, and life itself?

The reason why the early disciples came at last to identify Jesus with God was because they found that Jesus "worked"; that complete surrender to Jesus gave them unusual power. We are free to believe what we find within reason in the historical portions of the New Testament. Not long after Jesus went away, Peter and John went up to the temple to say their prayers. As they came near the gate called Beautiful, they heard the lamentations of a man calling for help. He could not go into the court beyond the Beautiful Gate, but he could beg for alms. He could not get to God, but he could get money to buy bread. That was as far as life went with him. Perhaps the people going through the gate would give him what he craved. To him the two disciples looked just like all the other temple worshippers. As he began his begging, Peter stood and looked at him, saying, "Silver and gold have I none; but such as I have give I thee." Then comes what to me is the important fact of that first discipleship: "In the name of Jesus Christ of Nazareth, rise up and walk."

Why is it that we are not more concerned with doing the mighty works which Jesus did? And why is it that we are not doing them? What a pathetic lot we are! We fail so often. If the Church were functioning in the name of Jesus Christ of Nazareth, there would be no problem of politics or of economics or of sociology in the world. We are futile because we have denied the essential thing. We have been quarreling about the doctrine of the Trinity, about the doctrine of the inspiration of the Holy Scripture, about the matter of the Virgin Birth, about the physical resurrection, about turning water into wine. The real things we have not attempted, because we have not yet met Jesus.

There is only one way we can meet him. We must find him in us. "It pleased God to reveal his Son in me," wrote Paul. Until we have found him in our hearts, we do not know him. And if we are not doing the great work that the disciples of the first few decades of Christianity did, it is because we have lost the road to the heart of Jesus.

III

THE POWER OF THE RESURRECTION

How rich the world has been since that moment when Jesus, walking along the curving shore of the lake of Galilee, addressed a few humble men toiling at their nets, and said, "Follow me." How thought falters and the imagination fails as we try to recapture and describe that holy experience! No wonder that we are still confused with words and that our thoughts are like dark days with the sun occasionally peeping through! It is too much for us, and because it is too much, we shall always be clumsy and confused when we draw near to him or when we seek to communicate to others, either by our character or by our words, what we know.

We can know little of these things mentally. When we rely upon the processes of the mind, we fail; but when we rely upon intuition, when we let ourselves go out and up to the height of this unspeakable mystery, we understand, and we come back with a radiance, a gladness, a power that convinces men.

That is the story of discipleship from the beginning, and that is the reason why the Church has gone on in spite of its blunders and its mistakes. We can forgive those blunders because we are also making them. It is in the heart of the prayer which Jesus taught: "Forgive us our trespasses, as we forgive those who trespass against us." It is easy for us to forgive our ancestors their mistakes when we discover that we are continuing them. The mistakes are along the intellectual plane. Perhaps it is necessary for us to be humbled by the realization of those blunders in order that we may be released to the attainment of such a spiritual resurrection that at last we shall begin to reveal in ourselves the glorious marks of the Lord Jesus.

St. Paul wrote the first letter to the Corinthians at a time when the gospel of Jesus was beginning to include the gospel about Jesus. We all agree that the gospel of Jesus is the fundamental thing, and that what we call the New Testament was an honest effort on the part of men to gather up the priceless sayings of Jesus;

as we are also agreed that they were bound to add their thoughts to his sayings. We have found further that Jesus did not establish a priesthood or a church as we now understand these words. But he did commit his gospel to the sacrament of living and of preaching. And Jesus still works more through the sacrament of living and of preaching than in any other way.

That is why, in spite of the anathemas of the Church, preachers and saints will carry on the gospel whether they are intellectually orthodox or unorthodox. It makes no difference what our intellectual reactions to Jesus are. A man may be intellectually sound as to a traditional dogma, and be spiritually damned. A woman may be outwardly right, and yet be in the heart of hell. And a person may be outwardly abandoned and wrong, and yet inwardly have the one thing necessary to salvation—the constraint of the love of Jesus.

The Pharisees and the scribes were not bad people as we think of badness. Many of them were heroic, and we owe much to them. We do not scruple to say that even Jesus owed the

Pharisees and the scribes a debt which he gladly paid on the cross. He loved them; he loved many things for which they stood. But there was one thing about them which he did not love—their dogmatism. That is still in the Church; it is the one thing Jesus cannot love.

Jesus cannot love the dogmatism of the Roman Catholics. They are wrong in their dogmatism. But we Episcopalians are just as wrong in ours. And it is the dogmatists who must be saved from the peril of Pharisaism. Let us be intellectually humble and admit that, after all, we know only a little. Perhaps nothing was ever said more greatly than Tennyson's cry, representing the renaissance of the new intellectualism in the nineteenth century, following Darwin, Tyndall, Huxley, and Spencer:

> ". . . but what am I?
> An infant crying in the night;
> An infant crying for the light,
> And with no language but a cry."

I wish it were possible at least for the Protestant Episcopal Church to be humble before the overwhelming fact of Jesus, and concede that no dogmatism concerning him is important. If the Church can continue the ecstasy of his life and the fellowship of his spirit, it will live.

On the other hand, we must admit that theories about Jesus were inevitable. It is impossible to meet such a life without trying to explain it. Luke wrote his Gospel probably a decade after the fall of Jerusalem. We believe that his first movement toward that Gospel was in the period of the imprisonment of St. Paul at Cæsarea, when Luke was in a position to gather important data concerning the teaching of Jesus and then the teaching of the witnesses about Jesus.

When St. Paul wrote to the Corinthians, he was beginning one of the first documents of the New Testament. The four Gospels were not yet in existence when he said: "Moreover, brethren, I declare unto you the gospel which I preached unto you, which also ye have received, and wherein ye stand." What was the gospel? To St. Paul it was two things: the death of Jesus and the Resurrection of Jesus. Of course, he included Jesus' gospel, but he added the gospel about Jesus. Jesus' death and his victory over death were the seal on his gospel. We cannot take the teaching of Jesus and live it unless we also accept the signature to that teaching. The signature is the shape of the cross and the ink is the blood which was shed upon it for the release of our human consciousness to the consciousness of our infinite Godhood.

When I think back to the moment when St. Paul was writing these words, I am overwhelmed by the unspeakable majesty of Jesus. I can understand glorious Luke, the poet and genius, coming upon some tradition about the Virgin Birth. He was trying, in that story, to explain the uniqueness of Jesus. When I come into the presence of Jesus, I know that with all his humanity, his humanity is different from mine. When I come into the presence of that perfect life, I can only fall at his feet, crying with Peter: "Depart from me; for I am a sinful man, O Lord!" I believe that the conversion of St. Paul was a real fact, for Jesus won me when I was only a boy. I know, when I come into his presence, that I have touched God. I do not know how. I only believe that in some mysterious way God at last found a man in whom He could completely become man; that, when that happened, somehow God and man were at last together.

All the centuries of Christianity have been struggling to articulate this. I believe that it has fallen upon our generation to make it a little clearer than it has been made before. It seems all the more wonderful and all the more divine that God should so bless the ways of ordinary people as to use them completely for His incarnation. I believe that God became man in Jesus; that God actually walked on earth; that God actually went through death on a cross; that God demonstrated, by rolling away the stone, that man is created to be immortal, and that He is calling him up to the heights of His own Godhood.

The men of the New Testament times were convinced that God had visited His people. Let us not judge the unbelieving world, but rather let us judge our unbelieving attitude toward Jesus and admit that we have been guilty of compromises; that we have not plunged into the pool of Bethesda with the *abandon* of the early disciples.

We know that there is no salvation from the things we hate until we meet Jesus. There is no use trying to explain him. Bunyon described his own former compromises and make-shifts when he told the story of Christian carrying the burden on his back, struggling, hampered, and then suddenly standing before a cross and finding release from the burden, which broke from his shoulders and rolled down-hill into the hell where it belonged. One thing we must know, that, about the year 50 of our era, one of the wisest of geniuses, one of the holiest of men, wrote these things: Christianity is a cross and a resurrection. But there can be no resurrection until on that cross we have been completely crucified.

II

No amount of wisdom or of inspiration in the words of Jesus could have affected humanity had it not been for the fact that he was greater than his words. If we take the words of Jesus and compare them with those of Socrates or of Buddha or of Plato or of Seneca, they are not sufficiently distinguished from the sayings of other masters. It has been said that in the words of Jesus there is nothing new. Scholars concede that the Lord's Prayer is a gathering together of pious phrases that are to be found in the devotional literature of the race out of which Jesus came. The same may be said about any great teacher. There is nothing new under the sun, except the teacher himself.

Consequently we must insist on the importance of Jesus. It is the Man of Nazareth who has made such words as "Blessed are the pure in heart; blessed are the merciful," mean so much to this race. And it is because of the Man of Nazareth that we stand at the door of all faith with Peter, saying, "To whom shall we go? thou hast the words of eternal life." But why is it that we think of him as having the words? Because, for the first time, a real doctrine of life was incarnated in a character that gave the doctrine a new force. It is the impact of the personality of Jesus upon the consciousness of humanity that makes the words so distinct and authoritative. To St. Paul the cross and the Resurrection were a signature by Jesus himself to the doctrine. Other men have spoken about the inwardness of the kingdom of God, but Jesus demonstrated it by his life.

The reason why we join with the writer of the Epistle to the Hebrews in "looking unto Jesus

the author and finisher of our faith," is because
he had joy in his life. It is the overwhelming
gladness of Jesus that impresses us as we draw
near to him, and sets him apart from all other
teachers. We regret that tradition should have
involved Jesus in notions of tears and sorrow.
We do not like the agonized face on the cross.
We see serenity under the stains of the blood
that drips from the piercing thorns of his crown.
We sometimes wonder if there ever was a moment when he felt that God had deserted him.
We cannot be sure that every word recorded of
Jesus was uttered in precisely that way. The
pious imagination of the disciples, inflamed by
the majesty of Jesus, was constrained continually to force words into certain situations of the
Master. It invites, of course, our sympathy when
we hear him say, "My God, my God, why hast
thou forsaken me?" It gives us comfort to identify Jesus with our moments of despair. Somewhere he was identified with such moments.
Somewhere he must have struggled up to that
height of understanding which made it easy for
him to say, "I and my Father are one"—but
surely not on the cross. There may have been

something like irresolution in the garden of Gethsemane, but again we must remember that we have only the witness of three men and, according to their own testimony, they were asleep most of the time while their Master prayed.

I see Jesus, after years of my uncertain following, as strong, as royal, all the way from that moment when he assumed the responsibility of his mission at the Jordan, saying, "It becometh us to fulfill all righteousness." There is one thing of which we can be sure, that, within a few years of his crucifixion, men who had known him in the days of his flesh had no difficulty in ascribing to him all that they meant by the word *God*.

Something which has always appealed to me is the fact that there is a letter attributed to one of Jesus' brothers, James. We know that, when Jesus was preaching, his brothers doubted him, and that Mary is revealed in the story of Jesus as being uncertain of her son's commission. We find words of rebuke again and again in that story, which do not fit into the theologies that have been so popular with the Church down to the present hour. Whatever we may think of the Blessed Virgin, she, with her sons, was not convinced, until after the cross, of the Christhood of the ever-blessed One.

But when we read this letter, attributed to James, which clearly represents what James thought about his brother Jesus, we cannot escape its implications: "James, a servant of God and of the Lord Jesus Christ." If only we could translate all this into terms of our own experience! Tennyson tried it in the *In Memoriam*, when he sang to his friends:

> "Dost thou look back on what hath been,
> As some divinely gifted man,
> Whose life in low estate began
> And on a simple village green?"

and went on to sing of him becoming a destiny that controls a throne.

Let us think of James looking back on Jesus, the boy with whom he had played. There is a reminiscence of Jesus' love of games in these words: "Whereunto then shall I liken the men of this generation? They are like unto children sitting in the marketplace." It is necessary for us to recapture the thought that a boy who had played with another boy, who had grown up

with him, who had joined with his brothers in
jeering at Jesus—as John in the Fourth Gospel
is careful to report—in his old age, wrote such
words as these: "James, a servant of God and
of the Lord Jesus Christ."

We cannot logically escape this fact. Something happened that set Jesus apart and that
started the doctrine of his deity. Suddenly men
began to think of God in terms of a Galilean
Carpenter. It was not all imagination. There
must have been obtruding and invincible facts
that constrained strong men in that generation so to write about a man like unto ourselves.

My answer is, Not the cross alone! Other men
have died heroically. And there are worse deaths
than crucifixion. When one realizes the awfulness of some forms of death, one thinks of Jesus'
hours on the cross as a rather fortunate termi-
nation of a glorious career. Some of the men
who came back from the war, maimed and living
still, can meet that moment of Jesus without
being abashed. No; it was not the cross alone
that lifted Jesus to such a height. There was a
victory. For the first time in the story of man,
the grave was opened and eternity was revealed.

It was that experience which made them cry, as we hear Thomas cry, "My Lord and my God."

When it comes to the simplicity of our faith, we are one with the cloud of witnesses who look with gratitude and wonder at Jesus, who for the joy that was set before him endured the cross. He must have known. He was not defeated. We are in harmony with St. Paul's conviction:

"If in this life only we have hope in Christ, we are of all men most miserable."

If our emotions are aroused by coming into touch merely with a man of gigantic character; if we are related only to the ethical life of Jesus; if our emotions have no more solid basis than the kindling from the contact of an inspired life, we are of all men most miserable.

We cannot leave the Resurrection out of the gospel of Jesus. Christianity is based on something more than an ideal seer and prophet. It is based on a fact of unusual power. And we hear a poet singing one of the most lyric stanzas in the psalmody of faith:

[69]

"Christ our passover is sacrificed for us: therefore let us keep the feast, not with old leaven, neither with the leaven of malice and wickedness; but with the unleavened bread of sincerity and truth."

That is the gospel about Jesus, and we must either take it that way or leave it alone. An ethical culture in terms of the inspired sagas of a Galilean Carpenter is not the faith about which these men were writing, for which they were living and for which they were dying. That first group was not stirred into its tumultuous action by anything less than a demonstrated fact that there are no dead and that man's soul enfolds the universe; that man goes on his way triumphant, from glory to glory; that the experiences of this life are only initiations, setting us free to that larger inheritance which Jesus possessed and demonstrated.

The gospel of Jesus does not stop with a thorn-crowned corpse. It continues with a radiant new life, a new beginning for the human race, a new point of departure, a magnitude of humanity that overflows all the creeds and all the songs and all the deeds of an historic faith, giving to those who possess it a new power, giving them faith in themselves in spite of their pathetic contradictions and their frequent disasters.

We like St. Paul because he registered these experiences. We understand a man who knew this fact and brought his life up to it, who was aware, as he came near, that there was something in himself that was dwarfed and unrelated; and he was ashamed and unhappy about it, and cried in humility: I do not for a moment pretend to have attained that height, but I press toward it. My life is a constant, conscious movement toward the height of the resurrected Jesus. I want no conception of God above the amplitude of that divine humanity.

To whom can a man go except to this mighty Releaser, this Saviour, and this Redeemer? He is not an invention. One of the most pathetic intellectual blunders of literature is the attempt to explain away the Resurrection by regarding it as the story of a deluded woman convincing the others that Jesus had really appeared. It is well for us occasionally to read over the fifteenth chapter of the first Epistle to the Corinthians, and remember that we are reading history contemporary to the event:

"I delivered unto you first of all that which I also received, how that Christ died for our sins according to the scriptures;

"And that he was buried, and that he rose again the third day according to the scriptures:

"And that he was seen of Cephas, then of the twelve:

"After that, he was seen of above five hundred brethren at once; of whom the greater part remain unto this present, but some are fallen asleep.

"After that, he was seen of James."

No wonder James called his brother "the Lord Jesus Christ." We should, too, if we were to come upon such manifested Godhood in a risen and victorious life. We should fling all our laurels down at his blessed feet and have done forever with subterfuges!

"And last of all he was seen of me also, as of one born out of due time."

We may share that birth of which Paul was proud, of which he forever boasted: He was revealed in me, and I speak of that which now I know. A belated birth mine, but still a birth. So we may cry: Born out of due time, too long being born into that great conscious victory, but now at last begotten,—with the echo of another one singing, "As many as received him, to them gave he power to become the sons of God."

That is the gospel *about* Jesus. We cannot leave the gospel *of* Jesus and the gospel *about* Jesus separate. They come together, wine and water, in the chalice of the new communion of an emancipated humanity!

III

When we read the first Corinthian letter, we discover that Paul found it as hard to keep his freedom as we find it to keep our own freedom today. People are people—but God is always God, and one has to make a choice between people and God, between the values of earth and the values of heaven. We must remember what the Master said in his gospel, "Lay not up for yourselves treasures upon earth . . . but lay up for yourselves treasures in heaven." We have no difficulty in understanding him when he speaks that way to us, for his whole life was a demonstration of the divine liberty of a son of God. How free Jesus was of anything like religious conventions!

We have no freedom in the Church today. If

we have any freedom at all, we have to fight for it continually. People seem to be persistent in their determination to rob their comrades of their freshness because they themselves have lost it, and because they have lost it, they are uncomfortable when they find it in somebody else. These words are not being addressed to the world outside but to the world inside, to the Church. We ourselves are responsible for the conditions that are existing now. We cannot understand freedom. We do not like it. We do not want freedom in the pulpit. The moment freedom comes and pours out toward us, we grow restless—and we would have done the same in St. Paul's day.

The important thing is knowing Christ in one's own right. If you meet a man or a woman in the Church who bears about in his body the marks of Jesus, stop criticizing him. You will recognize Jesus in any disciple—by tenderness, by selflessness, and, above all, by radiance. Not to be radiant is to be demonstrated as remote from Jesus; it proves that Jesus is not a reality but a speculation.

Is it possible to have the sense of the intimacy

of the presence of Jesus at all times? Is it possible for one to have the sense of that intimacy and at the same time reveal it in a changed life? Yes. But remember, the change is never sudden. When one studies the letters of St. Paul, one is bound to see how he kept growing to the very end. It was not easy for him to throw away the former man. That former man was a dogmatic, quarrelsome, narrow-minded churchman, haling man and women and children before the judge with the intention of death. But this man grew so tall spiritually that he was able to say at last, "For to me to live is Christ, and to die is gain," and to end his letters with the naïve and simple prayer: "The grace of our Lord Jesus Christ, and the love of God, and the communion of the Holy Ghost, be with you all."

No man could speak of God as a fellow, as a companion, had he not been walking with God. That is the fellowship of the Holy Ghost. No man could talk about the love of God unless he was overflowing himself, as St. Paul was when he wrote: "Though I speak with the tongues of men and of angels, and have not charity, I am become as sounding brass." And no man could invent, as he did, the phrase, "The grace of Jesus," without being himself increasingly gracious, bearing about in his personality all the marks of the risen Christ.

Our difficulty is that we are so far away from the event. If we can recapture it, we must practise it and manifest it all the rest of our days until our work is ended. One of the objectives of these meditations is to prove that the fact of the event is firmly established in history. These men were changed, not by a beautiful theory, but by a shattering experience. They saw God and man at last in one life. Had their experience ended at the cross, it could never have changed their lives. It was because the experience went beyond the cross, it was because Jesus did actually live among them, because they saw him and talked with him, because they were convinced in divers ways that man had at last succeeded in entering fully into the Godhood, that they began themselves to be changed. They were being constantly challenged by the height of that Resurrection.

Any one of us is a disciple if he knows the Resurrection, if his life is being manifested under the glory of that Easter dawn. That was the gospel of Jesus and that was the gospel about Jesus in the first century, when men were beginning to proclaim abroad in the world the fundamental truths of that life manifested in the ultimate victory of the open tomb. We must be set free from anything like ecclesiastical narrowness. We cannot go on into the heights of the resurrection if we are ecclesiastically limited. It is a fetter which we must break if we would walk with Jesus. We say to the whole Church: Break down this barrier against your freedom, and at the same time, remember that your freedom must be consecrated. Never make your liberty a cloak for maliciousness. Ask only that you may be free to express the gospel as it has been given to you, because it is by that gospel alone that you live.

We have had too many secondary, derivative disciples. We need more primary disciples in the Church, and we shall never have them in terms of a rigid ecclesiasticism. So far as a traditional theology is concerned, it must sit lightly on our shoulders.

Within a quarter of a century of the event, the companions of Jesus were announcing the fact of the Resurrection. Their lives were changed by it because the fact had entered into them. If our lives are not changed, it is because the fact is only in our heads. It has not set our imaginations on fire. It has not opened the barred gates of our hearts. And until the imagination is kindled and the heart is opened wide, there will never be authority in preaching or manifest divinity in discipleship.

The thing that above all things we crave is to be set free from the traditions of the centuries, to return to the simplicity of that hour when St. Paul wrote his letters, when he could speak triumphantly of his companions going out into the world, facing the hard, mocking, angry, wrong, malicious world, and overcoming it—not asking the world for certitudes in order to make their work easy, asking nothing of the world except an opportunity to manifest the gospel and to preach it in season and out of season.

Let the whole Church come back to that simplicity. Let us cast down our thrones and our principalities and powers. Let us dare to resist all tyrannies that thwart the humility of Jesus, the crucified and the risen Lord.

IV

THE RESURRECTION AND THE LIFE

In answer to those who say, "Why enter into controversial matters?" we reply, That has always been the way of the gospel. There is no escape. It is cowardly to seek to settle back for comfort's sake. Every one of us must go forward and preach, and we cannot preach if we are cowardly or insincere. Nobody can have Jesus unless he has touched the cross, unless he has shared all the sorrow that goes with it, and unless, in his own right, he has discovered what we are told the women discovered when the first Easter day was breaking.

What did Jesus teach? The only way to answer is to discover as well as we can the beautiful words he spoke, however overlaid they may be with the words of his interpreters who began to draw certain conclusions as to what Jesus meant and, in their effort to make the teaching clearer, often made it more obscure. People were so overcome by Jesus that they exaggerated him beyond humanity, which, of course, is good when we want to measure the height of Jesus.

We have seen that one of his brothers described him as "the Lord Jesus Christ." No amount of emotion or love could lead a man to say a thing like that, apart from an overwhelming experience. The overwhelming experience of the resurrected Jesus made it impossible for the disciples to think of him as they had thought of him before the cross. We found that they had thought of him as a great rabbi, as the last of the prophets. It had not dawned on them that he was Messiah or Christ. That we deduce when we read the Gospels themselves, particularly the story of the moment when the Master turned to his disciples and asked, "Who do men say that I, the Son of man, am? What do people think about me?"

"Some say you are a prophet. Some say you are Moses come back. Some say you are Elijah come back. Some say you are the last of the prophets."

"Yes, but what do *you* think?"

Then came Peter's answer: "You are the Messiah." Of course, Peter did not use the Greek word *Christ*, but the Aramaic word *Messiah*—

he used the language the Galilean disciples spoke, the language Jesus himself spoke.

The early disciples differed, naturally, as to what they meant by Messiah, "the Great Deliverer." To some people it meant delivery from Rome and to others delivery from the rule of sin. But whatever they meant by the word *Messiah*, toward the end of Jesus' ministry it began to dawn on them that Jesus was something more than man. When they saw him dead on a cross, they ran away. What happened to inspire those discouraged and defeated men and women in such a short time afterward to go before the whole world with the most wonderful story that has ever been told?

The one thing which has saved Christianity from the beginning is its loyalty to Jesus as supreme. Christianity has always fallen short of its purpose when it has philosophized about the nature of Jesus. We cannot philosophize about the nature of any man unless we accept him in terms of human psychology, and we must accept Jesus in those terms. And one is a coward or insincere if he will not face the issue, because the whole gospel of Jesus turns upon that.

[81]

There are people who grow frivolous over the movement of some teachers to do everything in their power to establish the real humanity of Jesus. It is a vital issue. If Jesus is not heart of your heart, and soul of your soul, there is nothing in the story. The story of the resurrection is the story of the adventure of all human souls. Once we understand that story, we shall never again be common to ourselves. Life will never be sordid to us. It will be starry, lyric, full of wonder, and our only dark moments will be in the confession, "Against thee, thee only, have I sinned, and done this evil in thy sight" —for by hating any one I have denied the thing you taught, the God in one's soul. By hurting any one I have done what they did to you, Master, so long ago upon that lonely hill. When I hurt anybody, I nail you again on that cross. When I repudiate anybody, I repudiate you. Your cross spells the salvation of humanity by changing it from the nature of the devil to the nature of God.

If we are to go forward with the mission of the Church, we must forget all that has happened since the last of the apostles died. We must recapture the simple Christianity of the four Gospels. We must not sell Jesus for the shining bits of silver of an ecclesiastical tradition. And if Jesus is not reviving us, if he is not sending us forth with power, it is because we have bartered him for a substitute. When I see what a traditional priesthood has done to the people of the Roman Catholic Church; when I see them cowering before the possibility of purgatory; when I see them bowing down before pathetic images representing Jesus, I hear Moses on the smoking top of Sinai, thundering with the voice of God: "Thou shalt not make unto thee any graven image, or any likeness of any thing that is in heaven above, or that is in the earth beneath." When I realize that all about us there are people who are entangled in the revival of the vapid stupidities of a mediæval superstition, I hear the souls under the altar crying, "How long, O God, how long? How long shall we offer humanity these old superstitions in place of the glorious Jesus of the Emmaus road or the tender Christ of Mary's garden outside the place where his body was laid to rest?"

[83]

We must join in resisting superstitions, **for Jesus' sake** and for the sake of the work. First of all, we must be joyous. The story is true. You will say, "What do you mean? Were they convinced in some mystical way that Jesus lived?" Some of us are psychic, and some of us have psychic experiences; and we are led to believe that there is such a thing as the communion of saints. But that does not explain Jesus. We must face the fact that Jesus won before he died. He had already made the statement—one of the verified documents which come to us through the Gospels—"I and my Father are one." Part of the doctrine of Jesus is this: that, if we could be identified with God as he was, all the things that he did we should also do. It is because we repudiate our life in God that we cannot do the things Jesus did.

But then you say, "Why did he die?" He died to demonstrate the gospel of the resurrection. Man's infidelity toward the soul at this hour forces us to realize that the one thing the human race needs in this century is the certitude of the reality of the soul. When we consider what our young people are learning in colleges and universities, there is no doubt about the fact that most of these young people have lost the sense of themselves as divine. The Church has not brought it to them. The Church has sent them away. They have lost faith in the Church. But if somebody stands out with power and brings them the gospel of Jesus, how they run toward it! They are as eager and as glad to receive it as Mary was in the garden.

Can we blame the boys and girls of America for not having faith in any sort of church that will not accept the facts of history and of science? Can we blame the boys and girls of America for not being happy in churches which are made up of such narrow-minded men and women that they will not even let one make a fly-leaf mark in a prayer book? The bigotry and the intolerance of a traditional Christianity are responsible for selling Jesus and robbing our youth of the right to know him in the ecstasy of the Resurrection.

That is why we insist that we must clean house. How pious we feel when we sing,

"O Jesus, thou art standing
Outside the fast-closed door,"

when we ourselves, by our attitude, are pounding nails into that door and keeping it shut. We do not want to hear the truth. Our people are afraid of the facts and throw their hands up in pious horror when what they call the great realities are assailed. The great shams are being assailed. We are pleading and bleeding for the great realities in which we believe.

The first thing we must do is to stop explaining away the resurrection. When you go into mourning, when you weep and wail because death has come into your house, you are denying the resurrection. Who is Jesus to you that you will not follow on and, in the moment of your bereavement, say, "I have seen and I know the resurrection and the life"?

Now we turn to a passage which does not belong to the original document in the Gospel of St. Mark. It was written in the second century, and added to the mutilated manuscript. It is important because it bears witness to the marvelous thing that happened and its results:

"And he said unto them, Go ye into all the world, and preach the gospel to every creature.

"And these signs shall follow them that believe: In

my name shall they cast out devils; they shall speak
with new tongues;

"They shall take up serpents; and if they drink
any deadly thing, it shall not hurt them; they shall
lay hands on the sick, and they shall recover.

"Then, after the Lord had spoken unto them, he
was received up into heaven."

How naïve and far away, but attesting to
that to which we would bear witness at this moment—the joyous and invincible fidelity of those
first believers. There was no sorrow with them.
They had to face "the lion's gory mane." They
did not mind. They had seen the resurrection.
They did not sing, "Art thou weary, art thou
languid?" They sang pæans to him who for
them had overcome their world.

"And they went forth, and preached everywhere." "They" did not mean a selectly or-
dained group of ecclesiastics. It meant every
one of them—the boys and the girls as well as
the men and the women. It meant that the boyhood and girlhood, manhood and womanhood,
of the first century was convincing the world by
the radiance and power of discipleship.

We have not got it. We know we have not. If
we had, we should not be quarreling with the

tendency of this century to be released from the stupidities of a blind and groping past. We should not mind what our friends think of us. We should be willing even to be ostracized from our social group. We should stand out and say: There is the resurrection and the life. I, too, have seen the Lord and from henceforth I must be obedient. I bow to no authority but to the authority of that invisible witness of the living Jesus in my soul. I, too, have ascended into oneness with the Father and through Him I am able to do all things.

II

Jesus is not always pleasant, any more than a parent is with a child. But we can always trust love. Whom love chastens, love has already received. It is inevitable, if we are to go further into the mystery of the kingdom of God, that we should all be corrected by experience, necessary that we should be humbled occasionally as to our thinking. We have seen that repentance means being changed from one kind to another kind of thinking. How limited our thinking has been! But we need not be sorry for that. It is in the process of life itself, here a little and there a little, or, as St. Paul would have it: When I was a child, I thought as a child, I spoke as a child; but when I grew up, I let go childish baubles.

The companions of Jesus in the Church are letting go the baubles. We have to think ourselves into the changing environment of life eternal. While God does not change, His manifestations change. They change in proportion to our growth, to meet ourselves as we grow. So we turn to a discussion of the victory of eternal man over temporal man—the demonstration of the sons of God while they are still in the flesh, over that lower vehicle which St. Paul called *soma sarx*, or flesh body.

Paul, more than any of the teachers in the New Testament, gave us a scientific vocabulary of the soul. He stated definitely that we have three kinds of bodies. There is the flesh body, which insists that it is the only body, and so leads us into a far country where we suffer until we realize that even the servants in our Father's house are better off than we. Then there is the psychic body. Many people have advanced from the flesh body to the psychic body. All geniuses inherit the psychic body. But it is not given to every one of us to resurrect into the real body, the eternal body, the spirit body. The Easter story is the record of such a resurrection, and it includes not only Jesus but the whole human race. It includes us and all those whom we think we have lost.

We are all familiar with the story told by the Elder of Ephesus. We will not enter into matters of textual criticism. It is enough to say that scholars like Canon Streeter and Doctor Bacon agree that this remarkable document was written by an old man in Ephesus toward the close of the first century. They also agree that the old man, when he was a boy, had known Jesus. It may have been written by John, the so-called Beloved Disciple; but the facts seem to be against it. It is now conceded that all the first companions of the Way were dead before the fall of Jerusalem. Of course, there was Mark but he was not a companion in the true sense of the word. He was not among those who were at first called. He was not an apostle. The word *apostle* describes one whom Jesus designated when he said, "I have called you friends. Ye have been witnesses of me from the beginning." These men were dowered with unique authority. One of them came later—and how we love Paul, with his ultimate witness of the joy and the fact of the Resurrection!

By the time the first century was closing they had all gone through the little portal. But there survived, according to modern scholarship as well as the tradition of the second century, one who had known Jesus in the days of his flesh. What a wonderful man he must have been! "By their fruits ye shall know them." We must feel the glory of this man's genius for writing. The older I grow, the more I am haunted by the cadences of his words. He never sinks. He is always on the summits of his thought. He does not disappoint us after we have taken a breath of amazement at the wonder of the prologue. He sustains the *motif* from the start to the conclusion. I know of nothing so stately, so convincing, as this sentence: "In the beginning was the Word."

He is introducing us to the timelessness of God, the timelessness and spacelessness of life,

life beyond any of its material manifestations. In the beginning was this vital purpose of the Infinite. It was not a chemical accident. It was not some mysterious, unconscious-conscious urge, as some of our recent philosophers love to state, but it was the very God Himself.

"In the beginning was the Word, and the Word was with God, and the Word was God. . . .

"That was the true Light, which lighteth every man that cometh into the world."

Every man who is born into the world is a spark of that true light. That light was fully revealed in one Man, but each of us is an adumbration of that eternal flame of the mystery of the God-hood. The story of Jesus, as the Elder of Ephe-sus saw it, was this: This Light was in the world in the Man Jesus. This Light has come to us all. This Light appealed to the same light within men. When we say *soul*, we are trying to de-scribe this light; when we say man is a soul with a body or bodies, we are accepting the fact that the Light in Jesus appeals to the light in us. It is because that light is already kindled in us that we understand him, that we love him, that we are unhappy because we do not love him enough or because we so frequently fail him.

Jesus, because he was that Light manifested fully in one man, appealed to the Elder of Ephesus; and by *Logos* or *Christ*, the seer was trying to describe the fulness of that divinity which is invisible man. It is conceded that the Elder of Ephesus was guided by the letters of Paul. He seems to have derived much of his thinking from Paul. The most creative genius of the New Testament is the derided tent-maker of Tarsus. If we could only realize what an inheritance we have received from Paul, we should be forever praising him. We should not mind his occasional lapses. We should remember our own and the lapses of thinking Christianity from the beginning. It was Paul who gave us this wonderful phrase, which we believe was the inspiration of the Logos doctrine in the Fourth Gospel: "Strengthened by his Spirit in the inner man." Salvation is the discovery that we are that inner man.

There are people who are disturbed when they hear a statement like this, that Jesus died to demonstrate deathlessness. The question naturally arises: But did he not die for sin? The answer is: The only sin is the denial of the inner man. The only sin is the agnosticism of people concerning their own divinity. Jesus, in dying to demonstrate the deathlessness of the soul, died that he might heal humanity of the one sin. He called it the sin against the Holy Ghost; and we are committing it until we have recognized the source of our own life.

So Jesus told the story of the prodigal son. We go to a far country when we deny the soul. Into what a far country modern education has led us! How few people really are at home with their souls! How many of us are reading books and hunting teachers to give us some comfort about death, when we carry the comfort in ourselves. The resurrection and the life comes that moment when we are able to say as Jesus did: "I am the resurrection, and the life." Each one of us is the resurrection and the life. We shall get nowhither with Jesus until we have his certitude of limitless living.

John, at the end of his life, looked back over the story of Jesus and stated it in a modern way. One needs only study the literature of the

Gospels of the first century to realize how modern and up to date this Gospel must have been to those who first read it. He met all the problems of the hour. He was thoughtful, widely cultured, and he had spent his life from his boyhood proving the principles of the gospel of Jesus.

The story which John told of Lazarus and Martha and Mary is like our story. There are some people who are fond of quarreling with Mary. They go out of their way to defend Martha, on the ground that Martha was a practical person; that mystics at best are nuisances; that it is more important to sweep the house, to prepare the meals, to wash the dishes, than it is to sit in meditation and learn of incarnate Godhood. If our children ask for bread, will we give them a perishable thing? Would we not rather give to every one we touch the security of deathlessness? And, if by meditation, if by facing the problems of physical existence, we can reach the certainty of Mary, whom Jesus chose for the gospel story of the ultimate victory, shall we not seek that way?

Martha, being a practical person, went to

secure help for her brother. She was not sure
of what would happen, but in her sorrow she
was desperate. Mary stayed home. She knew
Jesus so well that she was sure. Martha was not
so sure; but she was in earnest and she was
brave. She sought Jesus. The conversation between Martha and Jesus describes the sort of
talk that we have today concerning survival.

We have been through that. We have investigated phenomena, have sat in séances with
friends in dark rooms, witnessing trumpet
voices, ectoplasm, manifestations. We are not
deriding them, but they are so unnecessary,
when it has been completely demonstrated. If
we knew Jesus well enough, we should not need
to play with these toys. If we could enter fully
into the life of Jesus, we should arrive at that
moment, when, in the presence of the phenom-
enon of death, its varieties of manifestation, we
should be able to say quietly: But I am the resurrection and the life, because I am convinced
that death will not affect me. I am convinced
that it has not affected my beloved. She goes on
—he goes on—I go on. My soul is the centre of
my personality. I am more than mountains and

the bulk of universes. I am in my Father's house, and this particular room is one of important study and experience. I have met Jesus and have discovered that, though he will have other tasks for me beyond the sunset, there is only one task he has for me now. He does not ask me to be pious, to be conventionally good. He says, Seek first the kingdom of God and His righteousness, and piety and goodness and all the other things will be added. But do not regard these as of primary importance. He asks me to find the kingdom of God in terms of my capacity for love. As I love, I shall know. As I overcome the temptation to be angry or impatient with provoking people; as I stand, in my own right, captain of myself as a soul, I shall know all these things. It is the only way by which I can discover them.

There are many cults in America at the present moment. Though we are not derisive, we cannot help but smile when we think of them in contrast with the simplicity of Jesus' way. Some of us think that by deep breathing, or by saying, "Every day in every way I am growing better and better," we shall enter the kingdom.

But why feed on such husks, when the bread of life has been broken and given to you; when the announcement has been made, Now are you a child of God and an inheritor of everything that is God; when at the door Jesus' hand is tapping, as he calls: Let me in. Let me come into you with my way of loving. Learn that the hardest task is the one I am asking of you. The sternest discipline is now before you. Begin now. Do not ask questions about what happens after death. Do not be too curious about the other rooms. Be sure, however, that in this present room you are manifesting Christhood; that there is an increasing Christhood in your consciousness; and that you win only as you manifest love against every earthly irritation.

Rise up now before tombs and with the lifted hand of your Christhood say: "I am the resurrection, and the life."

V

COMPANIONS OF THE RESURRECTION

CLAIM your divinity! There is set at once before us the distinction between a primitive approach to God and a modern approach. The modern approach to God is Jesus. It was Jesus who opened wide the door of freedom to the human race. God is no longer a dreadful Being, to be supplicated and bribed. Yet it is strange how, through the centuries of Christianity, that idea of God has persisted and is apparently as strong today as it has ever been! Even our liturgy is not altogether healed of it. Hymns in our collection continue to reveal that old leprosy. Sermons still abound in denunciation of sin, and people are still charged to be purified of the sins of the body.

We hear much talk from outstanding preachers, as well as from clergy in groups, to the effect that this age is distinguished from other ages by its diminishing sense of sin. Jesus lost his sense of sin. He said, You cannot make me think sin. Which of you convinces me that there is anything in sin, that it has any hold on the human heart or consciousness? It is because you yield your divinity to the lower aspects of your physical life that you find yourself in a maze of prohibitions: You shall not do this, you shall not do that.

Jesus never quoted from books to substantiate his gospel. He never cited the authority of any literature. "Ah," but you say, "did he not quote scripture to the tempter?" We reply, Yes; the only way he could answer the devil was by quoting scripture. It was the devil—the spirit that forever denies—that sought to limit the mind of Jesus to texts, to books, to authorities. He wanted to get away from them. He said, The kingdom is not here. You do not need any authority, because you have found yourself; and until you have succeeded in finding yourself, you are like the prodigal son. You are among the swine. You are eating the husks. Why act like a servant or a refugee when in your Father's house are many rooms, and there is need for your kind of sonship?

The Pharisees were fond of quoting texts. They established their teaching not only upon quotations from the law and the prophets but also upon the authoritative interpretations—their tradition. We can never be risen with Christ until we get rid of all the clumsy apparatus of an antiquated method of thinking, which was oriented in a Mediterranean world. We are familiar with its cosmogony, its terminology; and we must resist the theologians who force that terminology on us. People are still fettered by it. They cannot go to Jesus because there are such barriers of words, builded through the laborious centuries, between them and that freedom which is called Christ.

When St. Paul wrote his letter to the Colossians, he was conscious of two forces frustrating the increasing Christhood of men. The first was theology and pious, churchly practices; the second was paganism. Our world is the same. If Christianity does not raise us to Godhood, if it does not make us at home in the universe, setting us free from all fear of anything that can hurt us, if it does not give us the sense of the glory of the liberty of the children of God, it is of no avail. There is glory, there is majesty and power, in the freedom of living in our

[101]

soul, in believing that our soul is sufficient for us, in believing that God is crowded into that soul, in believing that we need lean on nobody. If we are to be risen with Christ, then we must claim what lies above. If we are living on intimate terms with ourselves as sons of God, we are released from sin and death and have ascended to the right hand of God.

We need St. Paul and this message. So far as the life of religion is concerned, be free from any kind of traditional fetter. Use all things but do not let anything use you. Be free. Be released. But some may say, "This is dangerous." We answer: Mountain climbing is more dangerous than morass marching and yet, at the same time, there is danger in the morass. It is better to fall from a great height than to be sucked into the mire. It is better to be nobly a failure than to be ignobly safe. The quarrel we have with many people who profess the religion of Jesus is that there is too much fear in them. They forget that perfect love casts out fear. What is the perfect love that casts out fear? The love that died on a cross, in a man's life and body!

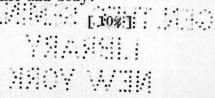

When the disciples of the first century spoke in that sense, they were thinking of the historic Jesus. Their words would have had no meaning without the background of the life of Jesus of Nazareth. It was he who made them realize the Easter message, which St. Paul so often repeats. My memory goes back to boyhood on the Magdalen Islands and late April, with the mayflowers laughing in the woods and offering incense to God, and the shy incoming birds singing; the quiet of a little church on the hill among the woods, the Easter music, and then the august, clanging words of Paul: "Christ our Passover is sacrificed for us."

Why was he sacrificed? The question has already been raised: Did Jesus die because of sin? Or did he die to demonstrate to man the sinfulness of being afraid of anything; that man, as a son of God, must not be afraid? There must be no fear, even of your enemies, of your traitors, of your detractors. Let them talk. They cannot touch you if you are risen with Christ. You may not be a miracle of perfection, because perfection, after all, is a relative thing. Nobody can judge how near you have climbed to God; therefore nobody is in a position to pronounce a word of judgment upon you. Be satisfied in your own heart that there is ascendancy in your consciousness; that your movement is upward. Even though there be blunders—and sometimes retreats—the urge of your life is upward. You are seeking the aboveness of life. You want the aboveness of the people you know. You are not interested in the things that other people say about your friends. They may be lazy and inconsistent; they may at times be exceedingly faulty; they may be neglectful of their duties; they may at whiles be fond of the pagan aspects of life—but there is something which still sets them apart, and that something is that they are always eager for aboveness. You feel, in their relation to you, that they are always bearing witness to the aboveness in you. They hold their enthusiasms; they are unaffected by your inconsistencies and your faults. They never take sides against life, but are always on the side of life, with all its failures, always ready to take up any cause with danger and reality in it.

Like David, how faulty! What a faulty man

he was, and yet he is spoken of in the Bible—and rightly so—as a man after God's heart. He wanted God; he wanted divinity; he wanted all the great aspects of existence. In spite of his inconsistencies and failures, there was an aboveness in the man that has made him loved through centuries—loved so deeply that, when Jesus came, they thought of him in terms of David, and called him David's son. It was the aboveness in Jesus that made them think of the aboveness in David.

Be unafraid of a traditional Christianity. Have nothing to do with it, so far as your identification with it is concerned. It is as dangerous and as ugly as paganism. Anything that has fear in it is a denial of God. Anything that makes your soul tremble in the presence of life is a sin against the infinite holiness of God's majesty. And we renounce in the name of Jesus any kind of preaching, any following of Jesus, that casts down its eyes and smites its breast. There is a time to smite the breast and to have downcast eyes; but not after you have met Jesus, not after you have realized he is living, not after you have discovered that you are one of his companions, not after you have discovered that the light of the world is flooding the human race, not after you have come to the sense of your own resurrected power, not after you have heard the Easter song: If you then be risen into Christhood, if you have come to be a brother of Jesus, if you are on his side, if you are one with all lovers, with all heroes and all helpers, go forward and assume your majesty.

On the other hand, as we hold no truce with a religion having fear in it, we hold no truce with paganism, which includes hate. One of the things that confronts us in this challenging hour is the awful laughter of those who live in outer darkness. I heard a young artist say not long ago: "It is almost impossible to make beauty today. The world seems to be made up of men and women who want to tear everything to pieces. Everything that is fine is being denied. People sneer at color, at form, at rhythm, at melody." There are devilish forces in paganism, and it is our joyous call to go through that dark world of gnashing of teeth, of bitterness, of serpent poison, without fear.

Beloved companions of the resurrection, they

cannot hurt you. Never mind what they say. You have risen. You have claimed your Christ-hood. You are a son of the living God. You are deathless. You are eternal. Climb from your flesh body through the psychic to the spirit body, and sit with Christ at the right hand of your Father which is in heaven. Seek those things which are above. Seek the aboveness in your own life, in your personality. Begin to live with the windows open toward your soul's highest, and let the winds of God bring you beauty and exultance and the assurance that you are most pleasing in the sight of Him who is singing above you as at the Jordan He sang above Jesus, "This is my beloved Son, in whom I am well pleased."

II

Jesus' word of truth is like sowing and har-vesting. Where the word falls on shallow ground, it does not last long, but at least it has received a sowing. Where the word falls on another kind of ground, with a good deal of rock in it, there, too, it must perish because the fowls of the air come and eat it, the briars and the thorns choke it, and the result is a withering and a loss. But sometimes the word is received by a soul prepared by life for it—a life that has been ploughed and harrowed, turned over and over by every possible discipline, a life that has accepted ploughing and harrowing. Then comes the harvest of the hundredfold.

The people in Corinth were like that, and people today are like that, too. So let us kneel before the truth in the well-worn saying which we must acknowledge: Life is what we make it. Nobody except ourselves can be blamed for the life that we live. Only laggard souls throw blame on environment or heredity. Brave souls stand up and acknowledge that whatever is faulty in life, whatever is unworthy, has its origin within one's self.

When we read Paul's letter to Corinth, we see that people were taking the story of the cross and of the Resurrection emotionally, but not rationally. Paul urged that our faith in Jesus is not an emotional, but a rational, service. It must enter into the reason. It must become part of the will. So we have heard the apostle sing, If you be risen, if you have accepted the Resurrection, let the aboveness of life be always your star. Be satisfied with nothing but aboveness— in people, in movements, and in your self.

Then, there were people who were taking the doctrine of the resurrection and were fighting about it. Some were curious; they wanted to know what life after death was like. We have all been through that experience. Some of us are passing through it now. We are interested in Jesus because we hope he will make us happy when we die. We want to meet our friends in the other world. We want everything exactly the same as it is here. We want to make permanent the things that please us. We are not stirred by the news of the resurrection because it manifests the love of God for the human race. We are not moved to confession and repentance when we read the story of a man who hung lonely on a cross and then rose again and opened the gate of death to every one of us. No; we are moved because we want to be happy, because we are egocentric.

When people ask me to speak, as they sometimes do, about life after death, they are asking of me the impossible. There is little information of value to anybody about what happens after death—physical death. But we have often quoted the old Hindu saying, which we believe ought to be incorporated in every creed: "As below, so above." For that reason, the Church wisely taught her children about an intermediate state, about purgatory, about hell, and about heaven. So far as this world is concerned, it has all these states. Hell is an historic fact. It is on this planet, and we know the type of man or woman who is living in hell. It is said of Judas, "He went to his own place." All hating and selfish folk are in hell. Jesus was so ardent with his gospel of salvation because he wanted to get souls out of their hells.

And if there are hells here, we may be sure there are hells beyond the so-called grave. Life changes our character, but death does not. When we die, if we are still in hell, we shall go to our own place. We shall not be affected because the soul is discarnate, so far as the flesh body is concerned. These hells last as long as the soul wants them. The soul makes its hell by denying God. God is love, and if we deny love, we deny God. If we deny love, we accept hate; and if we accept hate, we go to hell.

Perhaps the Church made a mistake in the Middle Ages in describing hell as a place rather than as a condition; purgatory—the intermediate state—as a place, instead of a condition of consciousness; heaven as a place, instead of a description of what happens when the soul is completely resurrected from every selfish motive. When we arise to meet the Lord in the air, in the aboveness; when we begin to be at home in all heights, when ideals become realities, when we throw everything away, are willing even to die, in order that we may be able to win the manifestation of those ideals, we ascend to the utmost heaven.

There are hells, and there are plenty of people today on this planet who are not only living in them but perpetuating them. You may visit hell any morning by reading the papers. You may find it right around the corner. And some of you may find it in your own homes. How universal was the scope of Goethe's genius when he described the devil as the spirit that forever denies! Have you cast out denial from your consciousness? Are you utterly released from shadows? Have you moved over into purgatory?

Are you glad about purgatory? Do you desire to be purged?

We must stop talking about what happens after death. Nothing happens. Nothing is changed. Souls are timeless. Souls are being educated. Souls are passing on from life to life, and from room to room. My judgment on this world at the present hour is that it is too lazy, too lackadaisical. We are missing what I think Paul meant when he said: Endure hardness as a good soldier. Fight the good fight of faith and lay hold on eternal life. If you be risen with Christ, seek always those things which are above. The trumpet will sound for every one of us. There will come a blast of experience that will shrivel us. We shall suddenly realize what pigmies we are!

In every friendship there is an intermediate state. On the one side is the hell of doubt and struggle, where selfishness is in conflict with selflessness; and on the other side is a dawning glory and wonder and amazement at the beauty of the other's soul. There are some friendships that have been completely purified. When Dante rises to meet Beatrice on one of the petals of the rose of God, that is heaven. This rose of God grows in the garden of friendship, and there are thousands who already live on that rose. There are lovers who have gone beyond all claims of bodies. There are friends who are so released that trumpets sound above their heads whithersoever they walk. Heaven is here and now. Browning was right in making Pippa sing,

> "God's in His heaven:
> All's right with the world."

All is well in any world when God is ruling it, and God is where heaven is set up by lovers.

Let God be in our heaven. Let heaven begin now. But it can only begin as we overcome selfishness. All the hells through which we have passed have been either of our own making or of the making of our friends. They have been made up of little acts of selfishness. We have been walking for years through the tragedies of bad people. And anybody is bad who is selfish. Anybody who is utterly selfish is a devil and makes hell.

But it is possible to pass through hells as

Jesus did. The Christ in us must descend into hell, must pass through the hells of his own and of others' making. If we want to enter the real resurrection of Jesus, we must be without fear. Do not ask for any amelioration of the conditions of your existence. The thing that holds you back is your demand for something better. Be like your Master, saying, The cup that my Father gives me, shall I not drink it? Loving your Father and believing in the wine of the kingdom, drink it—until the cup is empty and the golden bowl is reflecting the glory and the joy of your Father's face.

There is no difference between this world and any of the worlds of infinite space and time. Our beloved ones who have gone forth through the gate of death are not changed. They are as individual and as definite as you. All the beauty that was in them lives. They, too, must go on with experience until at last they have learned the way, the truth, and the life.

People have difficulty in reading St. Paul's letters because they think that he meant literally that there will be a last day, when a trumpet blast will shake the earth to its foundations and

make the graves yield up their physical dead.
He did not mean that. Paul used the apocalyptic speech of the first century, as the Greeks
used the speech of Homer and of Plato, as we
use today the speech of Whitman rather than of
Shakespeare. Every period has its own accent,
and great minds accommodate themselves to
that accent because they want to be communicated. They want to hand on what they have to
give, so they use the accent of the time. In
Paul's day the popular accent of poetry was
apocalyptic. Blake is the best instance in our
period of the apocalyptic method of genius, and
we must understand the method before we can
be intimate with the genius who uses it.

Paul did not always use it. How he changed
from the apocalypse of a judgment to this practical statement: "Concerning the collection for
the saints." He could come back from vivid
flights into the infinite, to talk about common,
everyday, important matters. We cannot find
the resurrection with Paul unless we direct all
our flights down at last into consecrated living.

We can be sure that the resurrection has
happened, but we are not so sure that it has

happened to us. Do you want to know when it has happened? "These signs shall follow them that believe: In my name shall they cast out devils." Are you casting out devils? Have you cast them out of yourself? Have you.cast out envy and selfishness? Are you no longer tortured by clinging to unnecessary things? Then do not be so eager to gain information about living in the isles of the blessed, or basking under a tree beneath a summer sky! Ask for the "wages of going on and not to die."

There is an ultimate victory for all souls, and it is expressed in a great hymn:

> "Christ shall bless thy going out,
> Shall bless thy coming in;
> Kindly compass thee about,
> Till thou art saved from sin.
> Like thy spotless Master, thou
> Filled with wisdom, love and power,
> Holy, pure and perfect now,
> Henceforth and evermore."

How shall we attain it? St. Paul answers concerning the collection of saints. There are things to be done. Begin building for yourself more stately mansions—the mansions of loving deeds. There are thousands about us who lack what we

have already gained. We can say to them:
What I have found of life, what Christ has
taught me, what my soul has accepted—I give
to you. And as we give, we gain; and as we
gain, we are glorified.

III

The glory of the cross comes from the open
tomb. The open tomb does not receive its glory
from the cross. The cross would have had no
significance apart from its victory. When men
began to enter into the consciousness of eternal
life in themselves, they began to see their cross
in the light of the glory of that knowledge in
them—which everybody wins by accepting Jesus
without debate. That is the message of the gospel
as it was preached by the apostles. These men
did not debate. They were convinced by the experience and they bore about in their life the witness. There is something deeply moving in the
story, told in Acts, of two men, with their backs
purple from the cords of the whip that flogged
them, going back to their friends, holding up
their heads like conquerors crowned by a victory.
And there is something as deeply moving in the

witness which we have in the letter written by
Paul to the Colossians, boasting about the suffering he had endured for his little group.

We need to find the bearing of all this upon
our discipleship. Once we are convinced about
Jesus, his way of life and its terminals, we are
committed to the cross. Theologians have so mis-
interpreted the cross. Whether Jesus said this or
no, it does represent the thought of the first
century: "If any man will come after me, let
him take up his cross." We have had too much
talk about the cross of Jesus and too little about
our cross. We have made the cross of Jesus
magic. There is magic in love, but not the kind
of magic which still exists in the thought and
the practice of Christianity. If we could touch
the cross as the disciples did in the first century,
we should be as victorious over our age as they
were over theirs.

This is how they touched the cross: In the
light of the risen life, they saw themselves as
Christs. Any being who knows himself to be the
eternally begotten son of God, is a Christ. Any
one who is convinced that there are no dead, is a
Christ. Christness is the consciousness of life

eternal; and to have the consciousness of life eternal, one must be willing to die in the giving of that good news. There is the secret of the power—or the energy, as Doctor Moffatt translates it—of which St. Paul boasts: "I labour for that end, striving for it with the divine energy which is in me." We cannot keep that divine energy out, once we know who we are. And that divine energy is loving the way Jesus loved.

Love is the only thing that can redeem a planet, because love is God, and only God can redeem a planet. But there are only a few second-born people in any age. There are thousands of pebbles but few diamonds. Beauty is potential but seldom completed in a world. The sons and the daughters of beauty must be patient, and their patience must be described by their cross. We fail because we are too irritable and impatient. If we discover that our ultimate sins are really of the nature of irritableness and impatience with people, then we shall rise with this new energy which Paul believed was the source of his power.

As you look back over your life, what has most wounded you? This, which Shakespeare de-

scribed as "benefits forgot"—the burdens that
the un-reborn lay on you. When people discover
that you have entered into the life of love, how
they trade on the knowledge! What nails they
pound into your hands and feet! What thorns
they press upon your bruised brows! How they
expect you to die that they may live vicariously!
Every power that you have won by struggle and
honest living, they demand as theirs. They will
use your energy without having any in themselves.

The world is—has always been—full of vam-
pires. But God has a way, and evidently this
planet is one of the thresholds which He has
blessed with the bloody feet of His Christs.

Jesus is not the only Saviour and Redeemer.
Wherever love is born and committed to the
care of the weak, we have the sign in the heavens and the sound on earth of his coming.
What we must try to do is to reshape our lives
to the principle of the cross; to admit that, because we have so freely received, we must freely
give; to commit ourselves to the truth that, as
God did not send Jesus into the world to condemn it, neither did He send us into the world

to condemn it. Let us no more be criticizing Christians. Let us no more be committed to any scheme of redemption that uses force. It is much easier to follow Paul's way of haling men to prison and shutting people up in jails, for morality or for public safety, than to accept a cross ourselves and be crucified to save people from their sins.

We shall have a hard time once we have accepted the resurrection. If our Christhood is to continue, it must go all the way of Calvary. It is a sin to put all the responsibility on Jesus and to take none of it ourselves. There is enough opportunity in this provoking, irritating world for us to practise our Christhood.

There is nothing in our Christianity except this, and if we have this, we have it all. That is why we keep pleading with the world to stop party cries, as Paul pleaded. We should like to say to the churches: Stop this talk of Anglo-Catholicism, of Modernism, of Fundamentalism, of Roman Catholicism. It is all so wrong. People who keep alive these party cries are denying Christ, whether it is one in high authority or but a doorkeeper in the house of his

God. Our only sin is to fail love, to run away from our cross, or to be suspicious of it. Let us rather accept the discipline with joy, and be proud that we have won to such height of Christhood that the uninitiated, the unregenerated, the unconverted, are behaving toward us as they did toward Jesus.

If you are being crucified in your house—and you will be if you are the only Christ in it; if you are being crucified by your friends, do not speak against it but, in the presence of the fellowship, show some of the bleeding marks of Jesus. You are now so sure of the resurrection, so convinced of the going on of souls, that you are glad to have a part in the regeneration of humanity.

The next time some one repeats an unpleasant story about you, do not let it hurt you. Think of the things they said about Jesus! Think of the things they have been saying about the apostles; of the mean things people still say about St. Paul! One of the things that shocks me is what even the clergy say about the apostle Paul. They do not realize the fact that he left his very skin all over Europe and

Asia; that he bled as he walked because of his eagerness to convince men of the power of the resurrection, and that it was the zeal to communicate to people the fact of the kingdom of God already in the midst of human society, which made him joyous in the fulfilment of his mission.

Be lifted up beyond all the waves of strife. Be free. Be released! It is something we can win together. Let us hold this above everything else. Let us practise it wherever we meet, our song being: Now is Christ—the Christ in me—risen from the dead and, for the sake of those who still sleep in the valley of hate and brooding despair and sorrow, become a kind of firstfruits.

VI

THE COMMUNITY OF THE RESURRECTION

The name of the first Church might well have been called the Community of the Resurrection. The church began as people who had shared that experience were drawn together to talk about it; by talking about it, to understand it, and by understanding it, to apply it among those who knew nothing about it. Wherever people are gathered in the spirit of that community, there is the one holy, catholic and apostolic Church. Whoever has that experience, in proportion to his knowledge, is a bishop or a priest or a deacon; but we are all ministers of the Community of the Resurrection. Wherever that knowledge has been revealed, there has been power; and where it has not been revealed, there has been loss of power. When people complain about Christianity, it is because they are missing the old ecstasy of the Community of the Resurrection. A church that is made up of people who have not met the resurrection is one in name only. But wherever the church in any community reveals this ecstasy and ardor of life, there is Jesus; there is the Church; there is God the Father, and God the Holy Ghost. When the open secret of Jesus is revealed to a man, what mysterious things happen!

Any group can make a church if the group represents resurrection-consciousness. We must accept that, and let everything else that bothers us go. We must never return to the weak and the beggarly elements. We will not accept any authority except the authority of a resurrection-consciousness. We will say to the critics of Christianity: "You do not understand the Church. You have not met the Church. If we could invite you to the Church that meets in the house of Nympha, you would kneel and pray. You would no longer criticize us. You would be on our side. You would be glad of this open secret of Jesus."

Then we should say to all gatherings of clergy and laity: "Stop your quarreling, in the name of Jesus. There is nothing in the matter of your quarrel that is worth debating. There is only one truth—Jesus; only one name, his name; only one fact—he is risen and become the firstfruits of them that slept. If you do not have it, you are not a Christian. You still belong to the world of paganism."

Let us ask ourselves some direct questions: Do I belong to this Church that meets at the household of Nympha? Will some Gospel, some great witness, come out of me? What good is my Christianity if witness is not coming out of me, if power is not being manifested in me? Let us stop fumbling at church doors for release from headaches and heartaches. Let us cease feeling for the fringes of vestmented authority, hoping that we may be able to creep past without the ordeals of initiation and so enter into the mystery of the kingdom of God. How glorious was Browning in *Prospice*, signing himself as one who forebore to creep past, who wanted to pay life's glad arrears! We cannot share the open secret if we are trying to creep past.

We have heard the story of the man at the Gate Beautiful. There are many people in our world who are crippled and impotent at the beautiful gate of life. They will never go through it. They will always be on the outside, unless one of us helps them. If our Christianity is not helping the lame at the Beautiful Gate, it is of no value. We have been helped. If we have the fact, we must go out and work. We must preach the gospel of the Resurrection. We must join the Church of the community of the risen life. We must not be identified with a religion that is made up of magical expedients. We do not need drinks for headaches and opiates for heartaches. We must go out and be healers and releasers. We who have stood in the presence of the risen Christ, who have seen him face to face, who have been permitted to put our fingers into his wounded side and hands and feet—what do we, lying impotent at the Beautiful Gate?

Like Peter, stand before these cripples of life and say: I have nothing to give in terms of the alms you are seeking. But I have a priceless gift, and I would share it with you. In the name of the risen Jesus, I bid you, rise and walk. I bid you to get up from your fear of death; to arise from your fear of love and life; to put on your royal garment; to be anointed and crowned. I ask you to take up your harp and join the choir, and sing the new song at the wide-flung doors of eternal day.

All this is in the spirit of Paul's letter to the

Colossians—the spirit of every letter that he wrote. If he ever quarreled with people, it was because they had returned to the weak and the beggarly elements, because their Christianity was not valid, was not vital. The test of validity in religion is vitality. If you have a vital religion, let anybody challenge its validity. Do not be worried about the questions some of the cripples will ask you, even as you stand over them. Bid them arise from their cramping beds and walk through the Beautiful Gate of the temple. Or, as Paul would have it, "Let Christian wisdom rule your behaviour to the outside world; make the very most of your time; let your talk always have a saving salt of grace about it."

What is this saving salt of grace but the truth of the resurrection? Your conversation must be salted with a cadence of joy. So Paul asks of us what otherwise would be an impossible thing—to develop zest for prayer. Prayer without zest, without the eucharistic note, is not prayer. Prayer that is not intercessory is of no value. Think of Jesus in the garden of Gethsemane coming at last to the ultimate prayer: Not my will, but Your will. Not what I want, but what You want of me. Do You want me to take this course, Father? Is there no way out? Could I not stay a while longer with Peter and James and John and Nathanael and all the other beloved ones? Could I not stay longer with the women of the flock You have given me? I had hoped to meet the faithful in the temple. I had hoped that Caiaphas would come down from his proud seat and that Annas would lift up his hands in welcome to me. The Church does not want me. It wants form, authority, tradition; but it does not want love. It does not want the freedom of love, of gladness. It wants dourness and sorrow. And so I must go the rest of the way alone.

There is no value in saying prayers unless our prayers mean guidance for service. If we belong to the Community of the Resurrection, our prayer will be: How can I communicate it? How can I prove it? Or, What has been wrong with me? If I have a sin, it is because I have done something that has interfered with my power to communicate this blessed secret—open to us but closed to the world. The only sin of which a Christian should be conscious is that somewhere, through his selfishness or through his lagging faith, he has failed to say the word —failed to go into the house of sorrow where there is lamentation. And there must be lamentation when death comes to people who have not met Jesus. We have met him. Why should not others meet him through us? We are encompassed about by a great cloud of witnesses who have all experienced the resurrection. How they want to work with us!

Does our beloved Joan still walk the earth? Do St. Catharine and St. Margaret and St. Michael walk with her? Are there mysterious radiances through the veil, to us who still survive in the flesh for the ministry's sake? Can we draw on the inexhaustible grace of the Community of the Resurrection in the Church Expectant as well as in the Church Militant? If that is true, we must decide today to be a different kind of Christian.

Are we at the point where we can answer any question put to us about the resurrection? Do we know it so well that we do not have to refer to books? We do not need books if we have met the risen Jesus. Paul did not need any books, neither did Peter. The world was convinced by a group of comparatively illiterate people who were accustomed to hard work. The things we have today, throbbing in us like the great heart of Christ, came from people whose hands were horny and ridged from manual toil. There is something wrong with a church that has to be propped by evidences. Though I do not quarrel with the spiritualists, there is something wrong with anybody who knows Jesus and needs to be convinced of the survival of the soul by the latest book on spiritualism, or needs to study even Madame Blavatsky in order to be convinced of the eternality of the self.

The world is wounded. We must go to it and heal it. Let us examine our own hearts and say, Do I really know this? Or am I still in the book state? Must I be convinced by some authoritative apologist, or can I take the Master at his word: Where two or three are gathered together in my spirit, I am in their midst. My Father and I will come to you. We will take up our abode with you. I will always be with you while you are doing my work in the world.

From now on a simplicity that is ultimate

dignity must mark our relations with the world. We are too reckless, too heedless; we do a lot of damage in our conversation, in our deportment; and we do interfere. People are lying at the Beautiful Gate of the temple. We can go in and out, but somehow we have failed, through something in ourselves that is wrong, to say with Peter, "Rise up and walk." It is a good thing if the experiences of life can humble us, and bring us back in devotion to him who has said, "Go into all the world."

II

The resurrection is not an isolated fact. Jesus has won a victory for the human race, but this victory cannot be shared by him with humanity unless humanity accepts the conditions of the resurrection.

That is one of the difficult things for us to understand. We are so familiar with our natural manhood and so unfamiliar with our spiritual manhood that we inevitably translate spiritual experiences into the experiences of what we are as physical bodies. Consequently the language of the New Testament seems impossible for our understanding, our acceptance, and our practice. It is idle to avoid the difficulty by reading that language into the fact of Jesus only. That is the mistake which has been made through the centuries and is the mistake we are still making—in talking about Jesus as though he alone were the Christ, in talking about the resurrection as if it were his event only, in talking of divinity as though it were something that he had and that we could not have, in speaking of "the only begotten Son of God" as applying to Jesus but not to ourselves.

When the Nicene Creed was formed, the Fathers made the same mistake. They did not see that what they said of Jesus must be said of all his disciples. Jesus is indeed "God of God, Light of Light, Very God of very God; Begotten, not made; Being of one substance with the Father." But so is every second-born soul. We, too, when we have entered into the Community of the Resurrection, come under the description of the Nicene Creed. They had not understood the teaching of St. Paul, and we also have missed it. But let us try to gain it now, by carefully studying the contents of the Epistle to the Galatians:

"The heir, as long as he is a child, differeth nothing from a servant, though he be lord of all;

"But is under tutors and governors until the time appointed of the father.

"Even so we, when we were children, were in bondage under the elements of the world"—

our physical selves, our carnal selves, our flesh bodies—

"But when the fullness of the time was come, God sent forth his Son, made of a woman, made under the law,

"To redeem them that were under the law"—

the law of the natural world, the law of physical consciousness, the law of the servitude to death—

"That we might receive the adoption of sons.

"Because ye are sons, God hath sent forth the Spirit of his Son into your hearts, crying, Abba, Father."

There is nothing here that contradicts the Nicene Creed.

"Wherefore thou art no more a servant, but a son; and if a son, then an heir of God through Christ.

"Howbeit then, when ye knew not God, ye did service unto them which by nature are no gods.

"But now, after that ye have known God, or rather are known of God, how turn ye again to the weak and beggarly elements"—

Why go back to the physical body? Why go back to the limitations of the flesh? Why not apply the resurrection to ourselves now? Why not say: I am risen from the dead and I too have become the firstfruits of them that slept? I no more can die, and as I live in the Spirit, I shall enjoy the inheritance of the Spirit? How like we are to this description: "Ye observe days, and months, and times, and years." And how well we deserve the rebuke of the apostle:

"I am afraid of you, lest I have bestowed unto you labour in vain.
"Brethren, I beseech you, be as I am."

Here Paul reveals that he thought of the Resurrection as the applied divinity of Jesus; that it must now be a part of our human consciousness. If it has entered into our consciousness, we need no further instruction. All we need is opportunity to practise it. Like Paul, we will be humble about our possessions and confess: I have not yet fully developed this. I have not yet fully manifested it, but I have begun. The rest of my life now is a pressing toward the mark of the resurrection. I will be satisfied no more with the limitations of this physical body. I refuse to come under the bondage of my body. Even when that body is ill or distressed; even when the physical plane is overpowered by the confusion of tongues, I will assert my Christhood. I will lay hold on this eternal life which is now my inheritance. Though I stand alone in a world of dead men, I shall be with Christ.

The title we have chosen is *Increasing Christhood*. Where can we locate that increasing Christhood except in ourselves? Where can we meet Christ but in ourselves? How shall we obtain the knowledge of the resurrection and the life except as we practise it in ourselves? Why come under the blunders of the faulty thinking of the past? Why not now be free? Why not ourselves manifest Christhood with his power? Why not ourselves be releasers and redeemers? What do we, lurking in the shadows? Why have we not accepted his command: "Freely ye have received, freely give"? We must impart our Christhood. We must spend the rest of our days in these bodies developing that Christhood, asking of the Master opportunities to serve him: Lord Jesus, be released in and through me. Let the holy light of your Christhood shine now in my humanity. Make of my personality a candlestick that it may hold that light. Make of me now such a towering personality of resurrected consciousness that I shall be regarded as a city on the hill of God which can no longer be hid.

The Church would sweep the world with that doctrine. It would brush aside all infidelity, all antagonism, all questions, all criticisms, and all scoffing. Of one thing we can be sure—that the time is bound to come when the dead in Christ shall be caught up into their Christhood and so meet the Lord on his altitudes. We will no longer return to the weak and beggarly elements of which all the quarrels of historic criticism have been formed. We, too, will do wonderful deeds. If we could be consistently Christed, we should be able to do, as individuals, the things Jesus did. Jesus laid hands on the sick and made them well; and if we are not doing that, it is because we have not yet accepted our Christhood. Our lives ought also to bear witness to God. People should be changed from the bondage of physical bodies to the liberty of the glory of ransomed and awakened souls. We know that it has happened. Every one of us has met a disciple in whom Christ was so clearly formed that there was no doubt about that resurrected consciousness.

We remember the story of the glorious priest, Father Damien, who lived for twenty years among the lepers. What a complete release of his Christhood! If all the rest of the Church were to become unbelievers, that pioneer soul would still awaken the world with a trumpet call of the resurrection.

Nothing has happened within the last quarter century in the world of social force equal to the miracle of Mahatma Gandhi. What a Christ in Gandhi! Think of the lonely, almost naked, little saint, overwhelming the council of kings and the governments of ministers by doing the things that Jesus did when he was here. We must not limit Christness to what is called Christianity. We must not limit the resurrection to what is called ecclesiasticism. It is the very power of God that overflows all the boundaries of our human race, and the witness is in the words of him who said, "Where two or three are gathered together in my name, there am I."

We must not waste our time shedding tears over the sorrows and the pains of Jesus, and offering prayers of thanksgiving to God for the thing that he did. We must go out among those for whom he died, who are living at our very doors. If he rolled away the stone from the door of death, we must also roll away that stone from the consciousness of multitudes of men and women who have no hope whatever in God or in the soul or in the certain destiny of man in the house of many mansions.

Whenever we read the story of a suicide, we should be challenged. How our papers abound in the records of people who, because of despair, break their bodies into pieces, not knowing that they have denied the central truth of our human race—life without limit, life in God, life so abounding in God that the gates of hell and the darkness of death cannot prevail against it. If, instead of reading books or hunting around for obscure evidence of life after death, we should find it in ourselves under the cross of Jesus, what things could be done, even today, as we go about our business. It is our duty to see to it that Christ is really formed in us; that when we go into our own consciousness, we come before the presence of Christ.

No man has ever possessed this with a greater clarity or a more joyous power of consciousness than the apostle Paul. That is why he stands apart from every other disciple of Christ and witness to his Resurrection. His letters abound in that one thought: Christ in me . . . Christ in you. You are no longer in bondage. You are free. Demonstrate in a world of death your deathlessness, and in a world of hate, your love; in a world of turmoil your peace, and in a world of ugliness your beauty. Let Christ be formed in you, now and forever!

III

When Paul was speaking about the natural man and the spiritual man, a great civilization was rushing down to its doom. Now another great civilization is again rushing down to its doom. The natural world-order is coming to an end, and the natural man is bringing it about

—and he cannot prevent it. The only saviour in the midst of humanity at this hour is the man with the mind of Christ. The world will not be redeemed by rituals, by creeds, by pieties, by ethics, by laws. It will be redeemed only by Christs in human consciousness. Until we accept this, we are in a parlous state. All preaching at this hour should be directed toward summoning, as with trumpet blasts, all the sons and daughters of God to the standard of Christ.

Only spiritually minded men and women can save this civilization from disaster. That is why the churches must be rebuked for their folly, in disobeying Jesus as Peter did in the garden of Gethsemane. Judged from the standard of mortal mind, Peter did the right thing. He had a sword; Jesus was in danger; morality, righteousness, truth, were in danger; so he took the sword and he smote. But it only embarrassed Jesus. It forced him to direct his spiritual energy to the small task of curing a servant's ear, when the energy that was in him wanted to enclose the whole world.

This message is uttered to the churches under the authority of the Spirit. Let him who has an ear to hear, hear what the Spirit says: Have nothing to do with force in the name of Christ. Have nothing to do even with law in the name of Christ. Stand apart from every manifestation of this natural world, and rely only upon the incorruptible inheritance of your Christhood. There is no sin so terrible as the sin against the Holy Ghost, and whoever draws a sword or uses force in the name of God sins against the Spirit. The Church of this land is sinning against the Spirit by seeking to bring about the kingdom of God by laws and statutes. Let the world have its police force, its armies and its navies, its judges and its lawyers; but let the inner, eternal world of the companionship of Christ lean only upon the truth of the cross.

Eye has not seen what God has prepared for those who believe in the Spirit. No mortal mind can measure the kingdom as we, who have already been born into it, see it. To the world outside, this will sound like nonsense; and if it sounds like nonsense to you, it proves that you have not been born again. You are still in natural consciousness. You have not understood, because you have not the mind of Christ.

[142]

Of what value is this mind of Christ if you do not accept it, if you do not believe that he alone is the conqueror, that his way is the only way, that Christianity is not a statute, is not even an organization? Christianity is a life, Christianity is progressive living, Christianity is the manifestation of an increasing Christhood among the disciples of Jesus. Let us get rid of all the by-products of paganism which persist in the Church despite itself. Let us be done with establishing any truth by threat, by the proclamation of doom. Let us ourselves be the gospel and its witness and the Christ whom it eternally proclaims.

The world can be saved by Christ and by Christ alone, not a Christ two thousand years old, but a Christ born into our hearts at this very moment, a Christ revealed as we go about our daily business, a Christ who shines through our changed manhood and womanhood, a Christ who demands attention because of our sudden, inexplicable gentleness, tenderness, humility, absence of the old arrogance, of the old self-assertion, of the old empty follies, of the old hatred and of the old tendency to say and do mean, hurtful things.

Eye has not seen, except the eye of the converted soul, the glory of having the mind of Christ, the wonder of no longer being uncertain, the majesty that comes upon us when we can say: No more compromise, but now and to the end, obedience to the constraining love of Christ. The world is hungry for this word. Men are becoming increasingly aware of the fact that life is a vain thing until it has been lifted to the height of Golgotha, and consecrated and anointed by the ecstasy of Easter.

We are baffled because we have pinned our Christianity and our religion to certain facts that happened in the first century. We have been looking backward overmuch, and we have been romancing overmuch even of Jesus as he was in the days of his flesh. He has announced to us the Christ mind, and if we have the Christ mind, we walk with Jesus. We do the things he used to do. He continues his incarnation through us. We must be the extension of the life of God among men. We must dare the things he dared and do the things that he did.

Of course, we cannot do it in a moment. An old disciple wrote these words, which measure some of the difficulties that await us as we take up the challenge of Jesus:

"If we say that we have no sin, we deceive ourselves, and the truth is not in us."

Not even by the suddenness of his conversion near the gate of Damascus, did Paul inherit consciously and overflowingly the mind of Christ. But how it grows as we follow his story. If, as a test, as well as a most certain joy, you will read First and Second Thessalonians, then the letters that follow, you will discover the expansion of the mind of Christ in a convert. At first, Paul was sure that Jesus was coming again in a week, or in a month, or in a year. Like the disciples he had the old Jewish apocalyptic idea of the second coming. But gradually the mind of Christ pushed that notion out from their consciousness. They began to enter into the timelessness of their inheritance until at last Paul was throbbing with that majestic hymn which must forever be on the lips of every second-born person: Though I speak with the tongues of men and of angels, I am nothing unless I have in myself the love of Jesus, unless

[145]

my heart aches for humanity as his heart ached, unless my heart encloses everybody as his heart enclosed everybody.

We have seen this gradual ascent of our increasing Christhood in Paul's witness to the Corinthians concerning the resurrection. We no longer believe in a physical resurrection. Flesh and blood cannot inherit the kingdom of God. As long as we cling to bodies, we shall die. As long as we accept and give reality to the animal man, we shall know the valley of corruption. But once we have risen into the consciousness of our eternal and spiritual selfhood, we shall know the resurrection.

There may have been some lingering, surviving fallacy in the mind of Paul when he wrote about the trumpet sounding and the dead rising, but we know, as we go on with him, that in time he came to see that the true gospel of the resurrection is conversion. When we enter into our eternity, we are saved. When we claim our Christness, we are redeemed. Not until we have made that claim, can we say with the certainty of the apostle: "By the grace of God I am what I am,"—a newborn Christ but on his way to manhood, a Christ who in this world faces a ministry of redemption among men and women and children, a Christ going gladly on his way to Golgotha, knowing that the Easter dawn is breaking above its heights.

VII

FROM THE DAMASCUS GATE

THINK of the journey from the Damascus gate to a Roman jail! Think, too, of all the adventures involved—adventures of discouragement and of defeat, of joy and of victory, all mixed together, from the moment of the vision of the face of Jesus and the sound of his voice and the conviction, until the moment of writing to a group of friends far away. O beloved Paul, our spirit is bowed before your spirit! In shame we confess our faltering, our cowardice, our unworthiness. You smite us with the white flame of your love for Christ. May our hearts be cloven asunder and made wide open to receive more grace for the ministry that will be ours until the day's work is done.

That is our thought as we try to retrace the journey that began near the gate of Damascus and ended in a Roman dungeon. All the story of Christianity is told in that journey,—our story, too. No one of us has missed altogether the conviction that Jesus is the Christ, the Son

of the living God. The joy of our companionship has grown as we have realized that Christianity is a continuing Christhood, that somehow
the Christhood of Jesus is continuing through
his believers and in them he always lives.
Though sometimes we deny him, he is there to
forgive; though we desert him, he comes quietly
after us, calling us by name until we feel the
touch of his crook and are once more within the
enfolding tenderness of his arms.

That is Jesus; and though they jail us, strip
us, beat us, kill us, we will not yield to the world.
With Paul, what other can we say but this word:
"For me to live is Christ, and to die is gain"?
No more can we think of life without him, for
we have found that, as life continues in him, it
gains in power, in dignity, and, above all, in
usefulness. By his grace we are what we are. It
is a wonderful thing that we have come to the
point where we have learned to forgive people,
to be patient, to be gentle, to stand up to perse-
cutions, to forego our old arrogant selves that
pressed so for personal claims. That is a great
joy, and we have a right today to the realization of that joy. We must not confine it to the

Roman jail only. We must not make it merely something in a picture or a hymn or a creed or even in an organization that in his name changes the social relations of men and women and children. It must be in *us*.

We wonder at any kind of Christianity that would rob individuals of the sense of their priesthood. It is a sin to rob any disciple of the consciousness of his increasing Christhood. We dishonor the disciples of the first century if we give to them something which we ourselves dare not claim, or if we give to any hierarchy in the Church a power that is not ours. This truth turned to fire the heart of Martin Luther. This truth is the tree of life whose leaves have been for the healing of the nations ever since that inspired prophet of God stood before the world with his mighty doctrine of justification by faith, that any soul is purified before God by its faith in Jesus.

Just now it is difficult for some of us to reveal our continuing Christhood to the world because the body of believers is so divided. But it was just as hard for Paul. Let us recapture these words, written from prison:

[150]

"I am imprisoned on account of my connexion with Christ, and my imprisonment has given the majority of the brotherhood greater confidence in the Lord to venture on speaking the word of God without being afraid."

Luther, Charles Wesley, Moody, Phillips Brooks, Beecher, Spurgeon, any one with his heart aflame with the sense of this dignity of his personal Christhood, through Jesus, might have written these words. And these words must describe us, too. We must develop a discipleship which gives confidence to souls that they may speak the word of God as they have received it, without being afraid. How we hate all ecclesiastical intimidations. How we despise the shams and the mockeries that scatter the flock of Christ as they are being scattered today. That is why we continue to plead for the simplicity of the gospel of discipleship; why we clamor over and over again: Never let a church cramp you; never let a creed cause you to go astray.

Let your sense of the gospel give encouragement to everybody else. Whatever utterance comes from us is authentic in proportion to its power to release those who hear us, from their dreads and their fears. Any sermon that does not set a congregation free from these things is not a sermon. There is no validity in preaching if it merely fastens more fetters on our souls. There is no value in preaching that keeps rubbing into people the thought: "How bad you are. How wrong you are." That is not the way Paul preached. Paul, in the spirit of Jesus, could thank God for whatever happened. He could believe, were he alive in the flesh today, in many movements of humanity that are regarded with suspicion by leaders in the Church. Let us, as far as we can, in the name of Christ, resist all negatives. If our Christhood is to continue, it must be in the spirit of him who said: All that my Father has given me, I have given you. As God sent me, so I send you. Go now into the world with the good news. If we could release men and women to the consciousness of their indwelling Christhood, all these things would be done in that spirit. If at this hour we could make our ministry more evocative and releasing, every crime of which this overwhelmed human nature of ours is guilty would be forgiven.

That is why I keep insisting that the churches should not be tied up with so-called reform movements. Let us have done with all scolding preaching, the spirit of finding fault with the nations. Let the churches release the Christ in the soul, and the Christ in the soul will redeem the world. For me to live is Christ, and death is only a drawing nearer to Jesus. It means the releasing at last of our Christhood, resurrected into the Christhood of our Lord, who once said to his beloved friends: When your period of training is past and your earthly ministry is ended, you shall sit on seats of power. You shall share the kingdom with me. We shall be a companionship of the release of the divinity in all things, until in the end God shall be fully manifested. So Paul seems to have understood Jesus, and that is the reason why there is the sound of drum-taps, of bugle-blasts and the clashing of cymbals in his preaching. There was such gladness, such conviction, in it. He had met Jesus, and there was no doubt in his mind about it. He had seen the resurrected Lord; there was no uncertainty. Consequently, death for him was only the opening of one more door into a still higher adventure with his Master. And that is all it is now for you and for me.

For the rest of the journey we must let everything go that interferes with the manifestation of our Christhood. There are many things that are well enough for the unconvinced world, but not for us. There has to be a definite apartness from the casual things of life, as far as we are concerned. Ours must be the Christ life. There must be nothing in it that does not sound like Christ, that does not look like Christ. It will not be easy, but it will be joyous and powerful; and even though self-imprisoned for his sake, we shall send out power that will give encouragement to all the world.

But our Christhood must not be fitful. It must be continuous—and it will be if we completely yield to him. I have spoken of healing powers. There is not one of us who has not at some time in his life had a sense of unusual power. It is in every one of us, but it is not organized because our life has not been continuously Christed. To the question, "How can my life be continuously Christed?" I answer, The New Testament will tell you. Study it again and again. Think of the great words in the Epistle to the Ephesians, "That ye, being rooted and grounded in love." To be Christed is to be Christ, the giver of the new commandment, "That ye love one another, as I have loved you."

Rule out of your life whatever is not of love. Wherever you are influenced by any emotion that is not the emotion in the heart of Christ as you have felt it, rule it out. Begin now to attain your majority.

Oh, may it be true of us that, when we come to the end of the journey, we may look back from our Damascus gate and say, "For me to live is Christ, and now dying is great gain."

II

We all want to continue our Christhood, because we have met Christ in Jesus. If it were not for the Christ of Jesus, the word would have no meaning. The word has meaning for two reasons: first, Jesus manifested his Christhood through suffering. We must also manifest ours through suffering. Secondly, he manifested his Christhood against death, by rolling the stone away from the grave and revealing his eternity. We must also manifest our Christhood against the fears that are common to people concerning death. If we have been risen with Christ, if we have accepted Christ, we must be witnesses of his cross and of his Resurrection.

Where we deserve rebuke at this moment— and we must accept it if we are to go on to a greater ministry—is in our failure, when death touches us, to bear witness to the resurrection. We can have no justification for tears when death takes away any one we love. We must stop our bad habit of wearing mourning, our unholy habit of tears and lamentations when death comes to us—and, of course, the only way it can ever come to us is vicariously, because death cannot touch us personally. It can touch us mentally, but death cannot touch *us*. We are eternal. We cannot die, but we may be forced to suffer the illusion of death. It is when some one whom we love passes out of our physical ken that we know the agony of dying.

Even Jesus allowed himself to experience that when he wept at the tomb of Lazarus. Though he knew that he had power to call Lazarus out of the tomb, he mingled his tears with an innumerable multitude of this human race, knowing the awfulness of the dark valley, the gripping fingers about the human heart when some one whom we love goes away from us through the little door called death. If we are to continue our Christhood, the next time some one we love passes on his way, we must bear witness to our belief that he passes on to triumph. Instead of overwhelming people with your sorrow, prove to them that in the consciousness of a Christian there is no death. If you are the one member in the family who believes in Christ, you must be strong-armed. Let the others weep. Let the others be overwhelmed. All those things are inevitable to unbelievers, but be you strong, radiant, bearing the burden of your broken-hearted mother or of your overwhelmed father or your shattered brother or sister. Stand in the midst of the dry bones that clutter the valley of decision—a white and a beautiful pillar of your faith in Christ crucified and risen from the dead.

Paul knew that the glory of the resurrection could only be communicated through strong souls. We must be strong souls. We are all charged to come over into our Christhood. The power of immortality in us will be proportionate to our power to soothe and comfort others with our faith. Whenever we are tested, therefore, instead of being overcome, let us lift up our eyes to God and say, "Thanks for this test. Thanks for this new and unexpected exercise of my spiritual faith. Let it all be handed over to the cause. You have given so freely to me. You who gave me Jesus Christ—the story of his cross, of his death, and of his Resurrection, with the witness of the centuries—I thank You for this opportunity to be numbered among the witnesses of the eternal Christ."

If modern Christianity has been supine, it has been due to the fact that, like the early Christians, it returned to weak and beggarly elements. So many of our churches have been made up of unprepared people. So many of our sermons have taken up unimportant matters, forgetting what Jesus said: "These ought ye to have done—not to leave the other undone," but you ought always to seek first the kingdom of God and his righteousness. The kingdom of God is the rule of Christ in human consciousness. Unless the rule of Christ is set up in our consciousness, we have not seen the kingdom of God.

It is a mistake to think that the communion

of God has to do with earthly piety. It has not.
Piety is important but it is not the objective of
preaching. Jesus said, I would rather have the
other things than this—let your righteousness
exceed the righteousness of the scribes and
Pharisees. There is a righteousness in the pub-
lican and in the sinner which is not in merely
pious people. Our churches should be noted not
so much for piety as for power, for the radiance
of belief, the stalwartness of discipleship, the
broad-shouldered people who can carry burdens
and who are not forever melting into tears. We
want more *hurrah* and *hosanna* in our preaching and in our discipleship. We sinners, who
cannot forget the terrible days when we were
under the dominion of sin, are now in a state of
exultance and of praise. We have heard One say:
Now go into the world with the good news. Dry
the tears in human eyes. Straighten the bent
knees. Cleanse the soiled spirits. Summon the
dead out of old, entombed superstitions and
fears, and give them the life that I have given
unto you.

That is what we are doing who mean to continue our Christhood in blessed Jesus' name to

the end of the journey. There is no doubt about what will happen to the world if the disciples will continue a joyous, healing, helping, resurrecting Christhood. Whenever you find yourself tempted to indulge in self-pity, sternly rebuke it: "Depart from me!" When you find yourself leaning on somebody else for sympathy and comfort because you have a headache, forget the headache and go into the soul that never has headaches. Never load anything on the back of your comrade. It already is breaking under its own burden. If you are to continue your Christhood, stand in your own strength and ask sympathy from nobody—but give it. Ask strength from nobody, but give it, for all things are now yours who have entered upon your Christhood.

We pass over the sensible directions which the apostle gave to Timothy and to his churches, though it is well for us to remember the much misunderstood sentence about money. So many people misquote it. Money is not the root of evil. Nothing is the root of anything, except the love of it. If your love is environed and circumscribed by money, it will bring you trouble. That is true not only of money but also of any ma-

terial thing. It may be love of family. Probably
we are less guilty of that kind of iniquity than
the people of the Old World, but there is enough
of it in America,—the people whose Christhood
is entombed in the tale of their descent from the
crew or the passengers of the *Mayflower*, the
women who have made a social fetish of being
daughters of the Colonial Dames. It is good to
be identified with all the high adventures of the
past, but the moment your love is found there
and only there, the moment your love becomes a
kind of arrogance and pride, you have lost your
Christhood.

Most of us are afflicted today because we have
denied our Christhood. If we live according to
the flesh, we shall of the flesh reap corruption.
We may be pious, but, if we are arrogant, we
shall have trouble to the end of the journey. We
all need these disciplines. If we did not need
them, our spiritual evolution would be on some
other kind of planet. But surely the planet to
which we belong must have been wisely chosen
by the Infinite Father for souls like us, who are
only in the making, who are on our way toward
the ultimate victory which is so beyond our

power to understand that we fall back again upon the inspired use which Paul made of the words of an unknown poet of Babylon: "Eye hath not seen, nor ear heard, the things which God hath prepared for them that love him." But it was Paul who added something that the unknown poet did not understand: But the Spirit hath revealed them unto us who have the spirit of God.

When we have the Christ mind, we know everything that is in Christ. When we have the Christ mind, we know everything that is in God. We need no books to tell us whether God exists. We need no lecture to explain to us the reason why we ought to believe in immortality. People outside may need it, but we who have met Jesus on the road to Damascus, who have been convinced by a crucified Christ and saved by a risen Lord, who have the consciousness in ourselves, do not need to go to any one. We do not need even to go to church, we need listen to no sermon. All we need to do is to become the church, to become the pulpit, to become the altar, to become the sacraments, to become, in every sense of the word, the triumphant witness of the truth of the resurrection.

There is no state of the damned so terrible as a young man or a young woman, an old man or an old woman, in doubt about life. How sorry I am for you who are not yet converted. How I weep over you when I think of the danger that is still before you, of the perils that are opening up; when I realize how you are going to be crucified again and again before you are risen into that inherited consciousness, which is yours by right. I could be willing with Paul to go back to that hell if, by going back, I could pull you out. You remember once, as Paul was writing to his friends, he said of Israel: I could be damned for their sake. If I could only bring them to see what I now see, I would be willing to go back to their blindness and root it all out again.

That is in every Christ. What a noble line we have in the Creed: "He descended into hell." Christs will descend into hell. This is a personal conviction, offered for what it is worth: Exceptional souls are they who have already attained their resurrection but have deliberately, for the truth's sake, come back into the imprisonment of the flesh in order that they might give to others what they themselves have so freely re-

ceived. What a romance Christianity is! What
a challenge to the hero in our soul the preaching of the gospel is!

Now, begin to fight. We must, first of all,
fight against our depressions. Be like Paul, who
said, "I forget what lies behind." We shall do
better work once we have poured everything out
at the feet of the Master, and really believe that
we have been forgiven. It is wiped out. Many of
us have been pleading to be forgiven our folly.
Let us now go out, completely released. All the
fetters are now off our hands and our feet.
Again I remind you of Bunyan's story of Christian's approach to the cross; how, as he drew
near to that cross, the burden was on his back,
but as he stood before the cross in contemplation, the burden left him and rolled down-hill into
the cave of hell, where the memory of our sins
belongs. Let the cross lift the burden from our
shoulders. Be clean, be released. Go out now into
your Easter with a new consciousness. Neither
circumcision avails anything, nor uncircum-
cision, but this new consciousness, this new creation.

This new creation is our Christhood. We shall

enter now upon the offices, the tasks, and the responsibilities of our Christhood. God has made us ministers of our Christhood and stewards of the mysteries of Him who has taken up His abode in us. Go forward with power, and do not be discouraged if on the way you are still tempted. We will not forget the way of him who staggered under his cross and fainted, needing help in that moment. We will not forget the weariness of him who mourned, "I thirst," or who, entering into a possible shadow of death for a moment, cried, "My God, my God, why hast thou forsaken me?"

If our Christhood is to continue, it must be tested all the way from the Prætorium to Golgotha, that it may advance to the victory over death, and then, in the end, to the certainties of an ascended life; for when our Christhood has continued to the end and we have vanished physically to be no more seen, those who follow after us will stand on the hill of our Christhood in amazement and in gratitude, even as of old on the hill of the Ascension the disciples watched their Master vanish beyond their physical ken.

PART II

THE MYSTERY OF INCARNATION

I

THE WORD MADE FLESH

WE know too little concerning the mystery of our being. Is man's birth accidental? Does it describe his beginning? Or is there behind it something that transcends all experience?

To whom shall we go for information? We go to the scientist. His answer is either through psychology or through biology, and that ends in pessimism. Our world is discouraged because it lacks information. Surely it is the business of religion to give that information to its votaries. If Christianity is a revelation, what does it reveal?

For many years we have been satisfied in the conclusion that Christianity encourages us to believe that somehow death is not the end of existence. But we must ask a further question: What is it that dies, and what is it that survives? We are all familiar with the manifestation of death, even as we are familiar with sickness and with the wasting thereof. We have watched the young grow old and the old pass into the Valley. Nobody seems to have come back to give us any information concerning the destiny of man. That statement will, of course, be debated. But I answer by saying: Whatever your information is concerning the destiny of man beyond death, it surely is of too private a character to satisfy anybody who does not have it. The Society for Psychical Research has been in existence for a long while but the majority of people, so far as this Western world is concerned, still laugh at anything like psychical research. The prevailing mood of the intellectual age is one of negation. If we consult our friends, we find that either they are hazy about what happens when death comes, or they are indifferent. Many people have schooled themselves to believe that, after all, the question is not important.

Perhaps it is not. That all depends upon our point of view. There may be something vulgar in this over-eager scrutiny of the mystery of death itself, but if it is vulgar, the great souls of this planet must be entitled vulgar. From the beginning of conscious thinking until now, men and women have ardently looked at the mystery and have wondered. Occasionally there have come into the ken of our thinking outstanding souls—souls like Jesus, naïvely announcing, "I am the resurrection, and the life: he that believeth in me, though he were dead, yet shall he live: and whosoever liveth and believeth in me shall never die." Why did Jesus make that statement? Either he was deceiving himself, or he possessed actual information. And so, if the attitude of the modern intelligent world is justified, this Jesus was a crazy man, a fanatic, and a fool—and Plato, perhaps the greatest intellect that ever throbbed behind human brows, was also crazy, a fanatic, and a fool.

Then, as to the origin of Christianity itself, this must be faced: It did not begin with an enthusiasm for a certain kind of life once lived. It began with a conviction that the life once lived was imperishable. Had Jesus died, as we think of death; had his disciples adopted the modern flimsy method of thinking, there would have been no Christianity. There are many worthy people of our day who base their Christianity upon the ethics of Jesus. I answer: The ethics of Jesus are of no account separated from his victory and his conclusions. There is much fine-spun debate about that particular thought. It must be met, and we shall hope to meet it as honestly as we can. The ethical life, apart from the fact of the soul, has no meaning. That is how St. Paul regarded it when he said, "If in this life only we have hope in Christ, we are of all men most miserable." Let us go to the Epicurean and decide that the best way of existence is to make the most of it: "Let us eat, drink, and be merry, for tomorrow we die." If beauty is not eternal, then any artist is foolish to follow beauty. If truth is not in itself eternal, every scientist is foolish to follow truth. And if goodness is not eternal, every saint is a misguided fanatic.

Consequently, our theme is of the utmost importance—the mystery of birth. How does it happen that this imperishable soul—if the soul be imperishable—occupies for a little period of time and space such an unworthy and unreliable vehicle as the flesh? Think of the period of time you were in a body before you knew that you were in a body. How many of you today can remember back to your fifth year of this incarnation? How much of your life have you held from your fifth year up to your fifteenth?

These studies are based upon the fourth and fifth chapters of the second Epistle to the Corinthians. These are selected because they represent the kind of thinking that was current in the first half of our Christian era:

"Hence, as I hold this ministry by God's mercy to me, I never lose heart in it; I disown those practices which very shame conceals from view; I do not go about it craftily; I do not falsify the word of God; I state the truth openly and so commend myself to every man's conscience before God. Even if my gospel is veiled, it is only veiled in the case of the perishing; there the god of this world has blinded the minds of unbelievers."

We know something about the material-minded man, the man who has ruled out mystery from his consciousness, the man who relies only on his processes of thinking, the man who excludes every element from his thought except the mathematical formula.

We need only to look around the world of today to see how blind most people are. Their indifference has blinded them. When a census was taken on the reaction of people to the problem of immortality, it was discovered that a large percentage of people was indifferent to

it; that they did not want it; that there was
nothing in the idea of the going on of the soul
to commend itself to their consideration. Life
was bad enough anyway.

That is a fair description of the attitude of
many people to the mystery of incarnation.
They do not care. The fact that they do not
care describes them and shows where they are
—low down on the plane of incarnation. They
have a long way to go. The consciousness of immortality is the measure of our growth. It is
something we attain; the consciousness of life
eternal is won, like character, through struggle.
It does not come in a moment. It is the reward
of living, and if we are not living in this way,
the door is closed to us. We cannot know, and
we must incarnate again and again before we
discover it.

I am not giving you my private opinion. I
am offering you what I honestly believe to be
the New Testament teaching on immortality.
The doctrine of immortality has no meaning
apart from the timelessness of the soul itself.
We must learn to readjust ourselves. Our thinking for centuries has been faulty. People have

been lazy or indifferent, or they have been afraid of the implications. We have often heard what people have said about this matter: "I do not want to believe this, and this, and this." That attitude is a description of the languor and the laziness of certain souls. If you have doubt about your soul, you have described your damnation. It is because you are a materialist; because you are so encased with your selfish practices and habits; because you are so inwardly and outwardly veiled and imprisoned, that you cannot break through.

This information comes only through a daily crucifixion and a daily dying. Only as we surrender to the gospel of love can we climb to the throne where love sits in glory. Most of us do not love, though we may think we do. That is a fact which we must face. We are selfish; or vanity rules love out. Our conception of love is all wrong. We love only those who are nice to us. The moment anybody begins to be disagreeable, we rule that person out from our love. We are exclusive in our loving. If we are exclusive in our loving, there shall come to us no high, torchlike conviction of immortality. It is won only by the complete release of the soul into the consciousness of God.

Look at the face of Christ. What do you see in it? A beautiful hymn is the answer to that question: "Love divine, all love excelling." The only man who ever had certain, authoritative information upon the soul was the Man whose love so resembled the love of God, the love of the universe, that Paul was able to describe that love as the glory of God on his face. The only kind of glory God has is love. We mistake God when we think of His glory in terms of omnipresence or of power or of omniscience. God has only one high quality, fixed and unchanging. He is the "Father of lights, with whom is no variableness, neither shadow of turning." He is always unceasing and outpouring love, and only as we resemble love in its unceasingness and its continual outpouring, do we stand in the presence of that immortality.

Let me assure you, with the witness of St. Paul on my side, that the way into the mystery of our presence on this planet in our particular body is opened in proportion to our ability to consecrate ourselves, from now to the end of the journey, to the life of love. We must rule out everything but that one thing. There is no other way. How well Jesus put it when he described the thieves who seek to climb over the wall of the knowledge of immortality. He said: There is only one way into this knowledge of your immortality. It is through the narrow gate. And it is a narrow gate—narrow in the sense that no one wearing conditions can go through it. It is unconditioned love alone that makes possible our entrance into the presence. We must be stern and unyielding for the sake of the truth that lies at the end of the path for those whose feet are upon it. The prize is infinitely precious, and we shall win it as we obey the law that opens the door upon the mystery of our incarnation.

II

So many people want exceptions in their favor. They have curious notions about the spiritual world, about God, about the soul. Because they have these curious notions they never find God. They find make-shifts, but they do not find Him. They think they have found Him but they are deceiving themselves. They never find spiritual reality. The nearest they get to it is what they call religion, but they have no spiritual reality. Conduct is not spiritual reality. One's conduct may be altogether wrong, and yet the sense of spirituality may be as clear as in the holiest of lives.

The Pharisees had a clear-cut idea of conduct, but think of living in the day of Jesus and missing him, as they did! They not only missed him, but they put him to death because they insisted upon a too narrow interpretation of life itself. Jesus was revealing man's inward dignity and beauty. The Pharisees thought only of outward dignity and beauty. Their dignity was correctness and their righteousness was regularity of conduct.

For that reason, Jesus said to the correct of his day: I know wrong people who will possess the dignity of their spiritual nature before you. Do not deceive yourselves. Being outwardly correct has little to do with the discovery. If you can only find yourselves in your Godhood, if you can realize why you are here, the rest will be easy. But until you make that discovery, the way will be hard for you. And the way is very hard. Even for those who have gone through the gate of initiation into the way of the Master, there are difficulties. Jesus described them when he said, Sufficient unto the day is the testing thereof. There is never any evil in the consciousness of a Christ. It is only in the mind of the lower man that evil exists. The higher man sees that what most people call evil is an ordeal toward a better understanding.

St. Paul knew that wrapped up within his body was a precious thing—so precious that once he faltered in contemplating it, and cried: "Eye hath not seen, nor ear heard, neither have entered into the heart of man, the things which God hath prepared for them that love him." There is nothing that God has prepared for you but your own innermost self. There is no heaven like the discovery of that innermost self. There is no power equal to the power that comes when you can say, "I am a son of God. I possess this treasure in an earthen vessel." A frail vessel of earth is the body, but the body is justified because of its content, and the content is something as precious as Christ. There is nothing in the Christhood more precious than our inner-

most self. We are incarnated that this inmost
self may be released to the conscious possession of its destined inheritance, the glory and
the power and the beauty of the Most High.

If we believe that, how different life becomes.
We no longer complain because of irritations.
We no longer are critical of other people. Once
we have found ourselves as we are, we are able
to distinguish between the outer vehicle and that
holy self. If this had been said twenty-five or
thirty years ago, the average congregation
would have been shocked. But something imper-
ceptibly beautiful has been coming into the
world since that time. It came to your preacher
in his early ministry, after he had read Ralph
Trine's *In Tune with the Infinite*, one of the
most helpful books ever written. Be in tune
with the Infinite—but it is your infinite self.
Be in tune with God—but it is God in you.

We wish to avoid anything like controversy
or debate. If we ever touch upon certain con-
trasts or oppositions to our idea, we shall do
it tenderly, hoping that the Spirit will guide us
reverently into the truth. But when I think of
how even Christianity itself has violated the

gospel, when I see souls all around me imprisoned and fettered—souls of people who go to
church, who are devout in their religion and yet
absolutely chained, without any understanding
of the mystery and the secret which throbs always through the message of the gospel and its
greatest interpreter, St. Paul—I am torn between a desire to be indignant with the leaders
and the supporters of the Church, and a tendency to weep over them. I find it easier to go out
into the pagan world and tell this news, than to
tell it to satisfied, conventional Christians. They
are so clouded and held by the traditions into
which they have been born and in which they
have been educated, that Jesus has a better
chance to communicate his mighty secret to
those outside, as he had when he was in the
flesh.

Therefore, we must face this one fact: All I
have wanted is within me. I came on earth to
learn to live with myself. I am in this particular
body, surrounded by these special trials, to be
initiated more and more into these mysteries
concerning my own being.

"I possess this treasure in a frail vessel of earth."

[181]

People will say that St. Paul meant some acceptance of the gospel truth. I say again, There is no gospel truth but this: The Spirit himself bears witness with our spirit that we are all that we mean by God, all that we mean by eternity, all that we mean by holiness. We are the children of God and so we are God's heirs. We inherit God's Godhood, God's character, God's Christhood. All that was in Jesus is folded in us, seeking to be released.

But we can be released only by the way of Jesus—"if so be that we suffer together with him, that we may also be glorified together." When I look back over the long distances of life on this planet, when I think of the eons that passed before man appeared here at all, I am prostrate before the mystery of the soul of any man or woman, believing that, when I take a little child into my arms, as I do for baptism, I am as near reality as the shepherds were when they knelt before the cradle of Jesus; that unless I can see the mystery of a baby, it is idle for me to bow before the holy images of a Christian tradition. Those images are of no value if they hold me from the mystery of any soul, and until I see the mystery of that soul, I shall never be able to live with people on this planet as with children of God, heirs of God, and joint-heirs with Christ. I shall never be able to learn why I am to be patient with some people, why I must forgive those who crucify me, why I must overcome all the prejudices which I have inherited from my peculiar environment and education, why I must be stripped bare, before I can enter into the mystery of the meaning of any human soul.

Until we find the way into the appreciation of the individual value of the soul, all that we do in the name of Jesus is sham and mockery. Everything in our modern education seems to have conspired with its fellow to rob young people of the sense of their own inner dignity, and no teaching of Christ is valid that does not lead us into this practical application of the mystery of the self, as it led St. Paul:

"I am simply a servant of yours for Jesus' sake. For God who said, 'Light shall shine out of darkness,' has shone within my heart to illuminate men with the knowledge of God's glory in the face of Christ."

Has God illuminated your consciousness? Are you fixed under the steady ray of that light? Why should you hold lesser things precious in comparison with this priceless knowledge, "I am God's child"?

Life will teach us that by all its tests. So accept the tests. People are constantly saying, "Can you not give us some evidence for the reality of God?" I answer, I can only offer you the witness of your own life. You carry the evidence within your self. It is because you yourself are denying that deep mystery that you go groping so heavily and so uncertainly. I plead with you not to go outside your soul for the knowledge. Be on your guard against all the nostrums that are offered. They are of no value. Life is your best teacher, and your immediate perplexities are only the throbbing of the knuckles of God on the door of your consciousness. God is saying, "Let me in." Take that which most annoys you and hear in it the sound of the voice of Divine Consciousness walking in the garden of your holy and divine selfhood.

Your life just where you stand now is in the plan of your soul. Work it through yourself. That is what St. Paul meant when he said, "Work out your own salvation." Ask nobody to solve your problems for you. Until life has taught you to carry your own burdens, you remain apart. But when you hear the challenge of the Master of Galilee: "If any man will come after me, let him deny himself, and take up his cross daily, and follow me," and answer it, you find the way.

III

The life of Jesus was lived, and ended on a cross, centuries ago. Was St. Paul using rhetoric, making the life of Jesus a symbol of that complete detachment which every son of God ought to reveal in his relationship with life? Or did he mean that we do not know Jesus until we share with him his kind of life? Is there something in a man like Jesus which we can catch? Is it native to a son of God to live the way he lived? Or must we think of the life of Jesus as unique, something once done, with its grace and benefits to be conferred upon the pious and the faithful?

According to St. Paul, Jesus' life could only mean the kind of life a man can live in the midst of men when he has resurrected from an animal to a spiritual consciousness. This resurrection is not possible until we believe that we have experienced in ourselves all that we mean by God. While we continue to separate God from ourselves, while we insist upon thinking of Jesus as a life lived apart from human experience, we cannot know this resurrection.

We are still in the speculative age of our Christianity. We are interested in Jesus because we are sinners and should like to be saved from the consequences of our sin—which have somewhat to do with a penal fire and an everlasting damnation. We shudder at the possibility of a cosmic Voice, saying, "Depart into everlasting fire." People have gone on believing that, and still believe it. They cling to Jesus because they hope that, by clinging to him, they will not come into such damnation.

If you are satisfied with Jesus, with salvation, in that sense, take it for what it is worth. I think I hear him say, "Where your treasure is, there will your heart be also." If you are living life, resting solely upon the strong arm of the Son of God, be content with the meager portion that will be yours at the end of your initiation. According to the faith that you manifested while you were incarnated, so let your future be. If you lived your life afraid of God, if you shuddered at the sound of Him drawing near, if something was wrong with your vision that made it impossible for you to behold the face of your Father, that be your concern.

But according to St. Paul—and according to St. Paul's great Master, Jesus—that is the worst kind of hell we can experience. As we ask ourselves: Is it not time for me to get away from this, to renounce it, to turn my back on it? let us hear Jesus answer: Except your righteousness exceed the righteousness of the scribes and of the Pharisees, you shall in no wise enter into the kingdom of God. Strive to enter in at the strait gate. It is hard. Rid yourself of every encumbrance. Stand in the nakedness of your own selfhood, or you will not get through. Enter into yourself. Find God in the awful solitude of your soul, and you shall have the open reward of your manifest Godhood. Thus Jesus taught.

Is it possible to separate this teaching of Jesus from the pious handbooks of tradition which have come down through the ages and which still get in our way? Is it possible to scrap every theory of salvation and say: I will have none of it save in the terms of Jesus? That life was given for me. What have I given back? What is it that you require of me, Lord and Master? Hear him answer: As my Father sent me, so I send you. Go into the world and love it as I loved it; serve it as I served it; forgive it as I forgave it. I have sent you into the world, not to find fault with it, not to condemn it. I have sent you into the world to announce to man the more abundant life of a son of God. Be concerned with no evil except the evil of man's unconsciousness of his own Christhood and his own divinity. Let life teach you. May you increase in the wisdom and stature of your divine sonship, and grow in favor and grace from day to day, as I did.

We cannot ask anything less of such a Master than to be like him. It is not enough to be a disciple. One must want to be a Christ. Freely you have received, as freely give. What are you giving back into life? We read these words now in the sense of what we have been discovering:

"Wherever I go, I am being killed in the body as Jesus was, so that the life of Jesus may come out in my body."

[188]

I want no mystical sacrament that assures me of release from some catastrophe on the other side of the grave. I want to be able to say with such an apostle as the man who wrote these words: By his grace, I am what I am. I find myself growing more and more into this consciousness. True, I do not for a moment pose as one who has gone on ahead of you. I have not yet apprehended. But one thing I do: Forgetting all these lower states of human consciousness, I now stand at the summit of my Christhood, and take my crown of thorns, if necessary, and my cross, too. Men will crown you with thorns. They will nail you high as they nailed him. Your father or your mother may be among your tormentors; your husband or your wife or your son or your daughter or your brother or your sister or your nearest neighbor or your closest friend—but that is in the mystery of incarnation. There is no other way of birth, and whoever tells you of another way, heed him not. There is no salvation but to have in one's body the kind of life that Jesus had.

Think of living forever in terms of Caiaphas

or of Annas! Do you want that kind of immortality? Would you have all your meanness and your bitterness of nature go on forever? Let life strip you bare of these things—and the life that you are living today will strip you if you give it a chance. But you cannot give it a chance until, first of all, you have the courage to accept your own Christhood, your own divinity.

Never be satisfied until all that you mean by Jesus is in you. Never talk about the constraining love of Christ until you are looping humanity with the shining lariat of your own immensity of loving. Let life torture you as it tortured him—but into resurrection. Then you will know something about salvation and heaven and life eternal.

The mystery of incarnation is that we should be born into a world like this, with bodies such as ours, with infinite possibilities of unfoldment; that all which was Jesus goes on forever in humanity. The life of Jesus is the life of God in any human soul. It is the business of Christianity not only to evoke that life but to manifest it continuously. Any other theory of salvation is beggarly and unworthy of our consideration.

This life is what the world needs now, and the world is getting it. It is pouring out everywhere among men and women and children. I see it even in the red stain of Russian Communism, in the movement of China to release herself through the discovery of her spiritual integrity and unity against Japan. I see it in Japan as well. I see it wherever men are struggling and groping upward. In all the mighty movement of man on this planet, I see Christ emerging—and here with us in America, a fine humility upon our wounded brows.

How well we have taken our beating! We built little men of straw and gilded the straw over with a thin wash of gold, and said, "These be your gods, O America," to find that nothing made in the image and likeness of humanity can ever satisfy man. He can only be satisfied by something in himself which is eternally in the image and likeness of God. We hold to Jesus and to men like him because they bear witness to the fact that the mystery of incarnation, of birth, of man on this planet, is the unutterable, inexhaustible love of God who so loves the world, this planet, that He gives it man—not any one man—but man, His only begotten son, God out of God, Light out of Light, Very God of very God, begotten not made, being of one substance with the Father. He commits this beautiful son, after the fire-mist and the planet, to the limitations of a physical body with its definite lower animal consciousness, knowing that in time that divine, only begotten, everlasting Logos and ineffable mystery of the being of the Divine One shall be manifested.

Find the joy of your selfhood. Kneel in adoration before the mystery and the wonder of your divine sonship, and then begin to live the life.

II

ON SECRET SERVICE

Is religion guess-work? People who are opposed to the methods of the religious life say that it is. They cannot believe that there is any evidence in support of the factors which make up the religious life. Instead of judging the people who dwell in the house of God, they find fault with the edifice itself.

People who believe in God in outwardness only depend upon the profile of that outwardness. If life is smooth and easy, it is possible to believe in God, to believe in Christ. But the moment there is a little pressure of the crown of thorns, God and the soul are denied. So many people are unaware of the reality of the inward life. They have not found themselves. I charge you with complicity against your own soul if you refuse to take up your residence in your conscious spiritual selfhood. You may climb as high as your brain and be satisfied to stay there. You may live with your culture and your refinement, but it will not help you. All that is in the temporal. The thing that is seen is the thing you respect, but the unseen you, the unexplored you—how you crucify and deny it!

Life has no meaning apart from the fact that it is a way-station. Your soul is going on. If you rule your soul out, life has no meaning. That is the reason why there are so many tragic misfits in our world. They will be tragic misfits until they have made that discovery.

St. Paul was not writing about a physical resurrection. He was not thinking about immortality as it is ordinarily understood. Immortality, the survival of the soul, of itself has no value. The soul cannot survive until it begins to live. Resurrection is the ascent of our consciousness from the outwardness to the inwardness of our eternal selfhood. If religion does not do that for us, we are under taboos. There is no resurrection apart from the discovery of our divine selfhood.

People will say, "But the Bible says Jesus rose from the dead." Yes; we should not remember Jesus if he had not risen from the normal dying states to the states of eternal, conscious living. His open tomb was in him. And until we have found that place of resurrection in ourselves, we shall, as St. Paul would have it, be sorry as men without hope. Christianity can only mean complete identification of human experience with the experience of a man like Jesus. We are either in that experience or we are not.

But you will say, "How can I share it?" We have already discovered that there are certain things to be surrendered. I know that I cannot appreciate beautiful music if I cultivate a bad taste for music by listening to cheap stuff and being satisfied with it. I cannot appreciate beauty in art unless there is a constant crucifixion and refinement of my taste. I cannot discover souls if I am content with vulgar people. I must know that there is such a thing as spiritual caste. I must, first of all, have established that in myself. My taste for people will be the measure of what I am becoming. If I would enter into this consciousness of life, I must ask myself: What kind of life is it? What is this life eternal about which so many things have been said and are being said now?

This is the importance of the programme of Christianity. It is where it is distinct from all other programmes. With all his splendor and dignity, Prince Siddartha Buddha did not quite ascend to that state of consciousness which we find Jesus of Nazareth occupying. We do not climb into the height of this Christ consciousness by overcoming desire through negation. We climb as we overcome all these negatives in ourselves, as we increase our positive power. Positive power is attained only as we become identified with love at the heart of the universe. That love has nothing to do with physical emotion. It is a deeper thing. It is more in the line of a confidence that goes with taste. How confident was Keats when he sang, "A thing of beauty is a joy forever." He knew that wherever people heard that, they would understand it if they had reached the same experience. How life tortured Keats! Yet he gave to the world unforgettable beauty. The torture was only lower down. In the height of his consciousness, released by his confidence in the eternity of beauty, he sang like a god.

Love is the principle of the universe. It is

not tied up with personality. It has to be initiated into and through and beyond personality. We must pass through personality, until we can say with St. Paul, "Love seeketh not her own, is not puffed up, doth not behave itself unseemly." That is a high state of consciousness. It describes the Christhood which Paul had in mind. He saw it in Jesus; but he did not mean that it must be identified exclusively with Jesus. That is where Christianity has often been wrong. It has set the Christhood of Jesus apart from the thought of man and said, "Here it is enthroned. You cannot get near it. You may come to it through his mother, or through some saint, or through some sacrament. But you cannot touch it." That fallacy must be denounced as often as necessary for the sake of the splendor that is your soul. Accept no compromise with your soul. That which you seek in Jesus is in yourself. Life will crucify it—but how it will be resurrected!

An initiate will not worry about anything touching human life. He has heard the great One say: On this planet terrible things will happen to you. But, remember, you are only passing through and up into your inheritance. You could not win it without this initiation. I have overcome the world, and you will overcome the world, too. The world can never possess you. It can never defeat you. Though you go alone, though men strip you bare of everything that you have, pass on your way undefeated.

It is your duty to be resurrected now into your Christhood. This particular society to which you have been sent needs your saviour-hood. The world needs your saviourhood as much as it needs the Saviourhood of Jesus of Nazareth. It is you who must be crucified. It is you who must be resurrected. You have no right to stand claiming release from your burden. In your soul is its honest necessity to go forth car-rying some other's burden. We offer you no easy way if you would come into the ascent of your Christhood.

We must stop whimpering and finding fault. We must believe that our soul is enough, that in ourself is all we need. This is not a doctrine of individualism and self-sufficiency. It is the doctrine of Jesus. It is the gospel of Christ. I preach none other. If you seek for evidence, go out in your own life, try it, and prove it; and you will say, "It is the truth. I have found that, as I try it, I can live it, and as I live it, I love it, and as I love it, the glory of God is being manifested in me. I find that I have power to change people's lives for the better. I am beginning to discover that, like Peter, I am healing by the very shadow that I cast as I go quietly by." If we could come into that power by living courageously, what majesty of attainment for us! It is within our power. Seek for nothing else. Be constrained by that Christ loving.

II

How meaningless life is when we are apart from the Son-of-man consciousness, and how, in a moment when we think not, that consciousness is manifested! We have seen it at intervals in our own life since we came here. We have heard about it in the lives of great men and women who have been here before us. We have found it to our uttermost satisfaction in the Old Testament and in the New, with their records of God-filled men and women.

Naturally we do not expect to have it in its fulness just now. But we know that we are on the way to it, and life itself is the road that leads to it. We are not concerned with the possible objections to this fact of the Christ mind. We only waste time when we seek to gain a point by argument, particularly concerning those things which belong to our inner experience. We know that the realities of life are determined solely by this inner experience. We may reason as much as we like concerning the possibility of a fact but we know nothing about it until we have lived and experienced it.

We cannot reason out the fact of God but we can experience that fact. And until we do experience it, it will always be a riddle to us. According to St. Paul, the natural man knows nothing about this mystery. The natural man does not perceive anything along the line of this God or Christ consciousness. But the true, the inner, man does.

You may say, "I do not know anything about this inner man. All I know is my physical self. I am compounded of physical properties. When those properties are rightly aligned and related,

I am healthy; and when they are not, I am ill. All that you have been saying is beyond me. It lies in the region of the imagination. You imagine it."

I answer: I experience it. I can only imagine what I experience. We cannot imagine anything we have not experienced. Imagination is something that happens through the inner consciousness by the building up, through memory, of things we ourselves have lived. We can put them together. Sometimes we put them together crazily and sometimes beautifully. A work of genius describes the putting together of these inner experiences into such harmony and perfection of design that it lives forever. We have described Keats' passion for beauty as something that lives forever. But if we talk in terms of Keats to the hard-headed people who deny the things we have been discussing together, they will repudiate every one of them. They will repudiate all art, except as it deals with form and technique. The poets of America are failing pathetically, with a few exceptions, because they do not really experience beauty. They are not living beauty. They are living ugliness. The body of their work is perfect but there is no soul in it. They know nothing about poetry, because they know nothing about beauty. They merely take the perfections of art and use them as vehicles for their whimperings and complainings. That is not poetry.

Nobody can find God, or the assurance of His existence or the understanding of His nature or the power of that nature acting in one's self, outside experience. Whatever we mean by God, it is the highest possible objective for the soul's adventure. God may be revealed in beauty, in music, in the harmonious social relationships of soul with soul. But God is more than all these manifestations. And if that be true, no amount of logic can establish the fact of God, any more than reasoning can establish beauty as Keats knew it when he wrote, "A thing of beauty is a joy forever."

If there is such a thing as holiness, surely it goes beyond reason. No man can reason out the idea of the holy. Life must teach it to us. We cannot derive any knowledge of it by study alone. The real saints, who were unique experts concerning holiness, could always communicate what they meant by that word. But if anybody attempts to write or talk about holiness unless he has first experienced something of it in himself, it all ends, as do the modern poets, in perfection of form as to the expression of the idea, without any knowledge of the idea itself—no content in the Grecian vase, an empty beauty. Better a crock that leans awry but brimming full of the immortal Falernian, than to have the perfection of the Grecian vase with nothing in it. Our life may outwardly be as perfect as art and study and culture can make it, but unless it contains the essence of an inward spiritual experience, it is empty. Nothing of value happens apart from our own capacity inwardly to experience it.

Love is a high constancy of ascending experience to reality in its most beautiful and durable states. Jesus meant that when he said to his friends as he drew them out of the cluttering crowd, "Unto you it is given to know the mysteries, but unto them that are without, all these things are done in parables," because mystery can never be communicated to without-ness. It belongs to within-ness. God cannot hear us unless we hear ourselves in the silence of our soul. That is why so many prayers are impotent. We are making the blessed Reality in likenesses and images, and so we miss the fact of God in ourselves.

A difficulty appears at this point. In this discussion of God as an inward experience there is serious danger of confusion with egotism. Jesus said, "Many shall come in my name." There never was a truth without a counterfeit. If you say, "That sounds like individualism," you have not touched the fact, nor have you voided my word of its authority. There will be no danger of what you mean by individualism when you have discovered that the awfulness of God and of the soul are the same. You will then see the awfulness of God in every other soul. You cease to be an individual. You become a companion of the Holy Spirit. You are in the fellowship of the divine Nature, and you salute men and women no longer as trees but as gods walking.

Many of the things that are said of Jesus have been covered up because of our tendency to be over-literal. Among them is the truth in

the story of the man who was given his eyesight.
Jesus touched his life and suddenly the man began to peer through the mist. "Oh," he said, "I
can see!" And then the great One whispered,
"And what is it that you see?" "I see men like
trees." The Master answered nothing. When the
mists were cleared away, Bartimæus saw men
as they are—gods walking. Most of us use our
vision in a limited, obscured fashion. We see
life only as trees. We see ourselves as something
with roots only. Think of seeing a tree as Joyce
Kilmer could see it—wearing songbirds in its
hair, lifting its leafy arms all day in rapture to
the great Companion! God can lead you only
when you have let Him step into yourself.

Jesus said, "I stand at the door, and knock."
What door? The door of your consciousness.
Open your thought and let what you mean by
Christ come into yourself. Bear the light with-
in yourself. The Light of all the world must
flood you with its abundant radiance!

If we read our Bible taking these thoughts
as our guide, what a new book it will become.
How time will be lifted out of its socket and in
the place of the guttering candle, will shine the

everlasting light of the consciousness of the indwelling Lord.

III

At the present time our spiritual self is inhabiting a series of bodies. A body is a vehicle; that which contains is a vehicle of the essence contained. Whether we believe in immortality or not, we are confronted by the fact, derived from experience, that we have continued to the present moment by inhabiting a series of bodies.

Think back to the earliest body you can remember. What a strange, helpless little body, the body of your early childhood. Have you a picture of that body? I have one of mine and, as I look at it, it is not easy for me to realize that I am still I. When I take the picture of that child and place it against one of my recent photographs, it seems almost impossible to trace any resemblance between the two bodies; yet I am still I. If I could recapture what was going on in my consciousness when that first picture was taken, I should discover that it was the same conscious selfhood which is occupying the older body today, one of the many vehicles my eternal selfhood has used in this present incarnation.

We know from experience—which is our only authority—that we inhabit many bodies in the course of an incarnation. It makes no difference how strangely old-looking and worn your most recent body may be. If you have any knowledge of your deep eternal self, you know without argument that you are still you. Whatever changes time may have wrought upon any of your vehicles, it has not touched *you*. Time will never touch you, for you are timeless. How do you know that you are timeless? Recall your happiest moments, your high episodes.

We remember life by its episodes and forget the rest. In the long run, we remember only happiness. We forget sorrow, because sorrow is only a shadow of ourself passing by. But joy comes always in the morning of the soul's timelessness. Jesus never spoke about sorrow as enduring. He recognized the facts of sorrow and of pain, but he attached no importance to them. He spoke always about joy. We hear him often saying, "My joy . . ." as we hear him also saying: Your joy nobody shall take away from you, because your joy describes your own eternal self. Deep within the grandeur of your solitary soul there is a joy that passes human understanding. "Eye hath not seen"—eye of the natural man; "ear hath not heard"—ear of the natural man—those moments of cosmic joy which are known only in our divine selfhood. It is there that we find heaven, that we find God, that we salute Jesus, that we are released from our limitations.

We must learn to take our physical body down from its old assumption of permanence. It is not permanent. Do not let it deceive you. You may go into that outer tabernacle to transact business—business you came on earth to do. But it is only a temporary residence. We can only understand this as we experience it. But my argument is that we all at times do experience the permanence of a spiritual selfhood.

Let me give you an illustration. I give it in tenderness and in reverence, but in confidence also that you will understand why it is given. Several years ago, the woman who gave me physical being died. The last thing we did together was to pray. Her dimming eyes looked up at me and her fading voice whispered, "Pray for me." For a moment I was afraid. What prayer could my lips form to help that beautiful, simple, holy life about to pass from the outer into an inner tabernacle? Then God whispered in my ear, and I said, "Mother, follow me." I began, "Now I lay me," and waited. There was a pause, and the fading voice whispered, "Now I lay me."

I went on, "Down to sleep." Again came the voice, "Down to sleep."

I went on imitating her old manner when she had taught me that prayer in my childhood, until at last I came to this sentence, "If I should die."

"If I should die . . ."

"Before I wake." "Before I wake . . ."

"I pray the Lord." "I pray the Lord."

"My soul to take." The voice was growing weaker and weaker, and it ended on this whisper: "My soul to take." After that, there was no voice. She passed over into physical unconsciousness.

The following day I was lonely and unhappy in my room, recapturing episodes with her; and they were all beautiful. I could not remember anything that was not beautiful about her life.

But I was unhappy and exceedingly lonely, when it seemed to me that the door opened and there came into the room a young woman of approximately seventeen years of age. She was dressed as for a ball, wearing the balloon skirt of the Victorian period, but she gave it grace. Two curls hung on each side of her face. I saw her dancing and was amazed. She was bobbing about the room in a stately old waltz. She seemed to be altogether unconscious of me. Then suddenly she seemed to become aware, and did one thing that Mother always did when she was very happy: she clapped her hands and ran toward me, and said, "Don't cry. I'm through. I'm through!" And then she danced up what seemed to me a pathway of light.

I did not understand it at first, until I recalled that she had once told me how, the night before her wedding, a ball was given in her honor. Then I realized that, before leaving the tabernacle of the body, she had done two things: the first was to pick up the first high episode in her life, the night before her marriage; the second was to remember the one on whom she closed her eyes in life while she prayed, "Now I lay me down to sleep." Two episodes out of her life which were the most important had ceased in time and had entered into eternity.

Logicians may place this kind of information under the scrutiny of their method and find nothing in it. The scoffers may scoff and the mockers may jeer, but some of us know. Paul knew. We know it, or we do not know it. And we know it only as we take off the physical and begin to put on the spiritual. If life is not teaching us how to take off the physical that we may assume our rightful lordliness, then we have not yet learned how to live.

As long as we insist on living only in the physical values, we shall suffer. If we are unhappy at this moment, it is our own fault; it is because of our stupidity or of our pride that we are so wounded. We are not meant to stay permanently in this physical body. That is why the material way of living is disastrous. People whose happiness depends solely upon their physical life are in hell, and how they are tortured! The only escape is through the narrow avenue of the Jesus-road. It is the road of the life of love. It is the road of sacrifice, not because there is any immediate virtue in sacrifice, but because somehow sacrifice is a habit that grows as we begin to take up our spiritual habitation.

We grow weary of the old cares and the old burdens. We no longer want to be hampered by the trifles that used to seem so important. How important it seemed that we should move in a certain set, that we should be invited into a certain group, that we should have its recognition! But as we grow older, all that passes away. We smile at it. We now regard those things as a growing boy regards the rattle, the ark, and the picture books on the nursery floor. Those things, those baubles, were necessary once, but no longer. Life has lifted us into our spiritual habitation.

Of course, there are old people who still cling to their toys—and there is no spectacle so tragic as an old man still clinging to his childish toys, nothing so disgraceful as a woman who will not admit that her body is growing old, who pretends she is still sixteen. But what dignity is on a woman who grows old honestly. How we love her beautiful acceptance of the fact that the

[212]

physical tabernacle is being taken down. What radiance of her everlasting girlhood comes through the waning years.

"I know that if this earthly tent of mine is taken down, I get a home from God, made by no human hands, eternal in the heavens. It makes me sigh indeed, this yearning to be under the cover of my heavenly habitation, since I am sure that once so covered I shall not be 'naked' at the hour of death."

We shall not be naked at the hour of death, if by gradual degrees we begin to enter into the beautiful inner pavilion of our spiritual habitation. Our thoughts are the material of that pavilion. Our states of mind, our practices, are all building it up. Build in the beauty of your thinking and of your speaking and of your doing, and by degrees you shall discover with St. Paul that only the thing that is not seen is eternal, that the set of your soul shows life's innermost importance, and that your loyalty to its direction is your noblest attainment.

Live your life in dignity and in beauty and without fear. God will not fail your high impulses. He will keep faith with you. Transact the business you came on earth to do through

[213]

this outer vehicle, the body, and when that work is done, you shall say with the same confidence as the Master, "I have finished the work which thou gavest me to do." For we have all come here on secret service and under the sealed orders of our King.

III

TRUST YOUR KINDNESS

MANY difficulties confront the seeker after truth—so much crude dogma, such overlaying of creed and ritual, such bondage of our popular ecclesiastical superstitions, and such natural reluctance on the part of devout people to dare a new way into the mystery.

We need occasionally to remember that St. Paul was not popular. He never has been. He described himself as the least, and he was indeed the last, of the apostles. But how confident he was even in his loneliness. What was the secret of his confidence? His discovery that all of Jesus was livable in a man's life, that one did not need to go outside of one's self to find Jesus. Because a man is God's son, all that a man finds in Jesus must ultimately be found in himself.

I shall never forget the quest I made several years ago to discover Jesus in his Palestinian sepulcher. From boyhood I had felt that somehow one ought to go to the Holy Land to find Jesus. I had been trailing the Master through the years by way of the hymns and the chants, the prayers, the creeds, and the practices of the Church. I had also been trailing him through the writers of the New Testament. I had enjoyed following the trail, and at last I took the way of Palestine. I brooded for a while over Bethlehem, the little town of his birth, and in the course of the following of that trail, I came at last to Nazareth. I sought him by the Lake of Galilee. Then one evening I returned again to myself, and there I found him as I could find him nowhere else.

That is the only trail. The others have their beauty and their value. They are good for us, but in the end we must take the trail that leads through our self. Until we dare that trail, we shall never find him. That is the point where our greatest danger lies; that is the reason why so many Christians at this moment are weak. They want a substitute Jesus. They refuse to believe that the only way into Jesus is through their personal experience.

My Christianity did not work until I took this inward trail. It is out of this experience that I am pleading with you also to have the courage to take that lonely road. It is a hard road, but there is none other. It is the road of your experience through life. Do not lean on anything. Strip yourself bare of all previous acts of faith. Be quit of all authorities. Call no man master. Lean on no church, no creed, no preacher. Lean only on yourself, and you will find Jesus.

I do not speak this out of my own authority. I speak it in the name of him who said, "Call no man master." Do not run hither and yon for helps when the only help is in your self—your life, your soul, your spiritual consciousness, your power to come to grips with your own problem. But if you do this thing, what a Christ, what a saviour, you will become! There is only one second coming of Christ: when he comes into us and possesses us, when we have opened our doors to him, and he has taken up his residence in us.

As long as our consciousness is in the outer dwelling of ourselves, we shall never find Jesus. If we seek to find Jesus in the outer pavilion of physical consciousness, he will elude us. As we go back over our own experience, we dis-

cover that the reason why he has eluded us is
that we have sought an objective Jesus. We
have tried to find him through our favorite
preacher, through our creed, through our sacraments. He has failed us because he cannot
meet us that way. He can only meet us on his
own terms, as between two sons of God. And if
we refuse our divine sonship, we cannot accept
his divine sonship.

Of what value is the divinity of Jesus when
we refuse our own divinity? Of what value is
the Christhood of Jesus when we ignore the responsibility of our own Christhood? How we insult him by thinking to find him in the outer
court of our life, of our consciousness! I remember when I substituted a sacrament for the indwelling Jesus. I thought that, by rising early
in the morning and fasting and going to my
church, and in reverence receiving a consecrated
wafer and chalice of wine, Jesus would enter
into me. He did not, and let me warn you, you
deceive yourself when you think he enters into
you that way.

Life is your sacrament. Life is your Holy
Communion. You yourself are the only priest.

Until you have accepted that truth, you will still quarrel with your neighbor and despise him, in spite of your sacrament. I have watched the Christians of the outer court, and I have found in them no abiding love, no overwhelming charity. They are still exclusive, incapable of communicating their saving power to those whom they pass by from day to day. They are still quarrelsome and vain and empty. "Not every one that saith unto me, Lord, Lord, shall enter into the kingdom of heaven, but he that doeth the will of God"—and it is the will of God that every one of us should be Christed by making the discovery from within. We must be absent from the body if we would be present with the Lord, and the only place where we can be present with that Lord is in our deep, eternal self.

We must be concerned with no other discovery. It is stated with lyric authority in Anna Hempstead Branch's great poem, *The Marriage Feast,* so little read and so little understood. You who know your Shakespeare will remember the saying of Polonius, "To thine own self be true, and it will follow, as the night the day, thou canst not then be false to any man." Our lives

are wrong because we are not true to ourselves,
because we have never seen ourselves. We have
accepted substitutes, objectives. We have made
idols in the image and the likeness of the only
reality, and we have followed after those idols.

You will never be happy until you make the
discovery. That is the only salvation. Let me remind you of what Jesus said: The kingdom of
God, the discovery of God, the peace and the
fulfilment of God, come not through any outer
practices. They come only through an inward
discovery of yourself as God's son. It is not
found by any attempt to locate it in a religious
practice, nor even in a moral code. It is found
only as you struggle from day to day to overcome your lower self with your higher self.

If you ask, "How is it possible to distinguish
between one's lower self and one's higher self?"
I answer: Watch your kindness. Trust your
kindness. Be more concerned with your kindness than with your goodness. If you will study
Jesus in relation to people, you will find that
he did not care much for conventional goodness.
I have discovered that the people who put the
emphasis on their goodness are narrow, hard,

intolerant, and mean. They are tyrants, cruel, oppressive, always trying to make others come under the rule of their petty tyrannies. I have seen "good" mothers and fathers drive their children to desperation. I have seen "good" people in the church make the church a hissing and a by-word. Their goodness was of no value. It was full of a dry-rottenness.

Suspect your goodness, but be reverent toward your innate kindness. Practise it in season and out of season. Believe in it above everything else. Be confident in your kindness. Your kindness is a ray from the central glory of your self, which is the living soul. Your kindness is your eternal self, trying to go out into the outer court of your physical consciousness to transact your Father's business. Your day will try your kindness. Your relationships from the hour of your rising until the end of the day, and then into the night, will all sound trumpet calls to your kindness.

When you fail your kindness, you deny Christ. When you turn from kindness to unkindness, you crucify that Lord afresh and put him to an open shame. Trust only your kindness.

Do not trust even your intellectual conclusions or your religious practices. But trust your innate courtesy, that sudden softening of your heart, that ability to forget yourself, your rights and your wrongs, in pity for your neighbor, his problems, her needs.

All this came marching through the thought of St. Paul. He was not desiring to get rid of his body that his soul might have a play-day in paradise with Jesus. Your soul is your paradise, your soul is your heaven. Your soul is your Christ and your God. Find your soul. Practise your soul, and then you will have no doubt about its reality. You will not go to books to discover the meaning of your soul when your soul momently is giving meaning to your conscious existence, when your soul is guiding and controlling you, when your soul is standing at ease before its own judgment seat.

Though I love the art of the ages, I wish we could destroy all the false traditions in which the beauty of art has been manifested. I wish we could destroy the wrong doctrine of the traditional Last Day, with souls naked and frightened, cowering before an awful Christ on an awful throne; and substitute in its place the mysterious indwelling Christ enthroned deep in the soul's self, passing sentence on all our thoughts and all our acts. Stand before your soul and let that soul judge you. Let your innate kindness say to your outer hardness, "Depart from me into the hellfire prepared for all that is devilish and damned. Depart, you suspicion; depart, you tendency to hurt; depart, you grasping meanness."

Your enthroned Lord Christ will have conquered, and in the spacious citadel of yourself there shall be nothing except that which is written in the Lamb's book of life. Whatever makes a lie will be forever gone. Think of the immaculate state of your soul when a lie can no longer enter into the presence of that eternal judge. Think of taking up your residence now in your inner self. Think of the radiance pouring through all the streets and avenues of your indwelling Christhood out upon the world. Think of the cooling stream of the river of the water of life pouring into the hard, thirsty places of the world, giving to men and women and children the everlasting water of renewal!

II

Our chief difficulty is in divorcing our thought from a traditional, objectified Jesus. It is hard to let the Jesus of tradition go. The Jesus of tradition never lived. But the Jesus of history and of experience has been walking with mankind ever since the Galilean days. When he first came on earth, people insisted on relating themselves to him in terms of their idea of what he ought to be. He was to be a statesman, or a king, or a worker of miracles. But he was no one of these ideas. The disciples failed him because, when they came to understand what Jesus meant, they were incapable of following through. That has been the trouble with Christianity ever since. That is our trouble. We are not ready to follow through. We can serve King Jesus, Jesus of the crown and of the scepter. But can we serve Jesus of the basin of water and of the towel? How far are we and Jesus identified in that glowing service of any man or any woman or any child? We must judge ourselves by that alone.

It is not easy for us to think that what we

mean by Jesus and by the soul, or the self, are intimately related in one communion and fellowship. It is not easy for us to understand that he came to earth to show us the way.

Man finds it difficult to be resurrected into his deep, eternal self. The world of desire, the world of form, the world of space, the world of time, is forever threatening him, and yet man will never be fully manifested until he has overcome that world of illusion. That is why the mysterious divine self we call the soul is incarnated. The world is a testing place that the soul's true worth may at last be proved to itself. Jesus knew this truth, and in the fulness of time he manifested it in his own life.

The crime of conventional Christianity is that it separates Jesus from humanity. It is the crime of theology, of ecclesiasticism. And until we face that truth, we shall never be set free. We shall still be saying of the extraneous things of our religion, "These be thy gods, O Israel." This mass is your god. These sacraments are your gods. This church, this prayer book, this Bible, this preacher—all these are your gods—the artificial things, the unrealities which we have

set up in the place of the Most High. We have
committed the great sin and we are suffering.
There will be no forgiveness for us until we
have had the courage to emancipate ourselves
from our gods. Nothing can save us from ourselves but ourselves. Until we have entered into
the sanctuary of our self, we shall know the
outer darkness, the torment of the flame that is
never quenched and of the worm that never dies.

There is nothing in Jesus that is not in us,
and until we bow down to the Jesus in us, our
lives will be frustrated. We shall have no peace
on this planet. We shall wander to and fro and
up and down on the earth, without any power of
decision. Some of you have a crucifix to which
you kneel and say your prayers. But the crucifix cannot hear you, cannot save you. People
think that by signing themselves with the sign
of the cross, they have some mystical approach.
That is all magic. It is no higher than the taboo
and the animism of savages. "Thou shalt not
make to thyself any graven image," said Moses,
when he came down from the mountain and discovered that people were deluding themselves
with gods made from their trifles—when all the

while the salvation they craved was in them, the power they sought was dammed up and waiting to be released through their life.

Of course, some of you may say, "But you deny Jesus." In tenderness I answer: No, Jesus is important to me because he has by his life made clear to me that a man can bear about in his body all his marks and his characteristics. I do not want salvation until it comes to me in terms of my own power to serve people. I do not seek to be released until the power to release others takes its place in my consciousness. I seek the steadfastness of that power which Jesus had when he said, "I, if I be lifted up from the earth, will draw all men unto me." I know that if I can only lift myself away from the outer courts of my consciousness, that if I can set myself free from the tyranny of this physical personality, that as I begin to take up my residence in my deep eternal self, my outer self must obey and must respond.

We must judge ourselves by the way we live. Is it not true that nearly all our judgments are based upon external things, that our liking people depends upon whether they have the kind of eyes and face that we like, upon the tone of their voice, upon their grace and charm? But the outward appearance tells us nothing. There are many glittering, charming people in the world today, but inwardly they are full of hate and malice. And there are rare saints of God who carry burdens in meekness and in humility, whose holiness is hidden from all eyes except eyes that have been opened by the touch of Jesus. Our standard of values must be shifted from the external to the internal. We must know people by the quality of their souls.

As we look out upon our social order, we see that people are forming their judgments solely by the outwardness of this world. We speak of So-and-So as being brilliant, and So-and-So as being powerful and convincing. But we are indifferent to what inwardly regulates that life. We are so harnessed to form, to externals, to the outward, that we have lost our standard of values.

I have described my attempt to find Jesus by going to Palestine, by looking for him in old churches, beautiful hymns, appealing rituals. And then one day I discovered the real Jesus

by taking the hard, upward trail into myself.
There I found the thing you find—that kindness is your only standard. No soul has value
without kindness. Cut yourself apart from
everything that is cruel or hard. And you will
find that your kindness will open a gate into the
trail that will lead you to the realization of the
indwelling Christ.

III

Nobody can find the meaning of the Galilean
Carpenter until he discovers that there is something in himself that loves and understands the
Carpenter. That something is the soul, the son
of God—pure immortality, pure Godhood—
lonely, unhappy, until it has found a way to express itself in human relations. Let this mind
be in you which was also in Christ Jesus who,
being in the form of God, did not regard the
Godhead as a prize exclusively to be enjoyed,
but poured that Godhood out and became obedient.

St. Paul had become obedient. So every disciple becomes obedient to that in himself which
loves and understands the Galilean Carpenter.

However lovely, however divine the life that was lived, we dishonor that life until we discover it in ourselves as our utmost passion and our consuming desire.

We begin, as we have found, by practising our kindness, by renouncing every impulse but our kindness. St. Paul was not deceived when he said, "Fight the good fight. Lay hold on eternal life." Fight against the cruelty and the hardness of life, to save your kindness. Learn to be gentle, learn to be kind. Whatever stands in the way of that gentleness and of that kindness is evil. You yourself must discover in your own life this Christ of the reconciliation. Your forgiving word, your patience, the gentleness and the understanding of your gesture, are the outpouring of that which makes the Galilean Carpenter eternal in the consciousness of man.

Read the story of St. Paul—one of the most beautiful stories ever written—from the time when he was standing by, nodding his head with a cold glitter in his eyes while the enemies of Jesus stoned young Stephen to death. Paul's religion of goodness as such made it possible for him to stand by with folded arms. Watch him from that moment, until you see him on the Damascus road, saying: My God, I have been persecuting You. This was Jesus in myself, and I did not give that impulse a chance to save Stephen. I stood there and consented to his death. How blind I was!

That is the real story of the conversion of Paul on the road to Damascus. It is everybody's story. One day it will be your story. It was mine. Somewhere on the road of life I learned that only kindness counts, that nothing else is worth while. I had been taught to believe that if people had a religion other than mine, I was justified in treating it harshly. I sneered at what I called their superstitions. I stood like a Pharisee, thanking God that I was not as other men were. Then one day I met the Christ in me on my Damascus road, and he said: I am Jesus. I am Jesus in you, and you have been denying and persecuting me. That is the story that makes the name of Paul sound like a peal of bells from the tower of witnesses, raised from the beginning, to the eternal reconciliation of God, in the Christ power of human consciousness.

This power is in the world now, more than ever. I know that if I had said these things some thirty-four years ago, when I began my ministry, hardly anybody would have understood what I was saying. But now I am conscious of the fact that everybody agrees with me. The reason why people look with criticism upon the Church is not that they dislike the Church; it is because they look in vain to find Jesus in the people who go to church. They can find him only in the loving kindness of church-people. If our church-going does not make us kind, then our church-going is folly. There is kindness everywhere in the world. There is kindness in the heart of people who go to church, and there is kindness in the heart of people who misunderstand the church and deride it. One day all this kindness will gather together, and "the earth shall be full of the knowledge of the Lord, as the waters cover the sea."

One of the encouraging things about humanity in the world today is that it is so ready for the Galilean. Some one has asked, "Is it possible for you to conceive how Jesus would behave in a city like New York, in the midst of people like ourselves?" I answer, Yes, because I have seen Jesus in New York. I discover a vast amount of Jesus among the people I meet.

Jesus could be indignant. He could thunder against the hard and the cruel, calling them a generation of vipers, saying to them, "How can ye escape the damnation of hell?" He was not thinking of a traditional Gehenna. He knew that the only hell is the hell which burns and foams in cruelty and hardness, that the only devil is the incarnate spirit of selfishness and of possessiveness which is active in so many people. He knew that they could not escape the awful consequence of the Gehenna in their souls, the Gehenna of hating, of selfishness, of cruelty. And how he thundered that day when he walked into the temple and saw what was taking place in a church—cruelty, hardness, contempt. His voice throbbed and pealed like a trumpet as he said, "My Father's house is the house of prayer; but ye have made it a den of thieves." No gentle Jesus about that, but a stern accuser of everything that is rapacious in the name of religion.

Jesus would have a good time, even in the city of New York. As he went up and down our

streets, he would salute all kind people. He
would disdain the hard and the cruel, because
he would know instinctively that they were not
ready for him, unless he found underneath the
hardness and the cruelty just a grain of kindness. One day he said—he called it *faith*, but it
is the same thing: If you had in you as much
kindness as a grain of mustard seed, you
would overcome the mountains of your cruelty
and of your hardness; you would be able to say
to everything that separates, "Be now rooted up
and cast into the boundless sea of God's love,"
and it would come to pass.

Paul once said, "When I was a child, I spoke
as a child, I understood as a child, I thought as
a child: but when I became a man, I put away
childish things." The time must come in everybody's life when he will say *good-bye* to all the
objectivities of a traditional Christ. My quarrel
with many people who follow Jesus is they never
follow Jesus in themselves. They are suspicious
of the Jesus in themselves. They want Jesus
in the Mass, in the sacrament, in the Church, in
the creed, in the ritual, in the smell of incense-
smoke, and in all the formal chants and hymns.

That is not the way to find Jesus. But we can find him in the city street, in the sympathy of our heart toward those who need his loving kindness and compassion, as we give to them that loving kindness and compassion. We must offer them the sacrifice of ourselves.

What a glorious sentence we have in our Communion service: "And here we offer and present unto thee, O Lord, our selves, our souls and bodies, to be a reasonable, holy, and living sacrifice unto thee." There is only one sacrifice —the humble and the contrite heart. It is a holy sacrifice when we crucify all our outer moods and attitudes toward the world, when we give up our claims on people, when we say, "I make no more demands on anybody. I have come into the sanctuary of my own selfhood. I have taken up my place of abiding in my deep eternal self."

Some of you may say, "What do we know about our deep eternal self?" I answer: Have you found no deep eternal self in life? Is life only on the surface? Does life consist only in the things you see and hear and taste and smell and touch? Is there not something in your life that has gone away, that is no longer outwardly visible? Does it die? Is it dead? Has sorrow taught you nothing? Is your love gone because the outward manifestation of its object is no longer visible? Is it not true that with every beat of your inward heart you are keeping faith with the one who has gone ahead of you? You tell me there is no deep eternal self. I answer: Your self, your loyalty, is that. Tennyson crying,

> "But oh for the touch of a vanished hand,
> And the sound of a voice that is still,"

is a witness to the reality of this eternal, inward, invisible self of our human consciousness, which we call the soul.

If you look into that self, you will discover that all your great impulses come from within, that your life has been guided mainly by that inward power. You cannot see the power, but you can feel it. That is why Jesus said to Nicodemus: You must be born again—you must be born from your outer to your inner consciousness.

Then Nicodemus said: But that means nothing to me.

Jesus answered: Are you a master in Israel and do not know these things? Let me tell you, Nicodemus, the wind blows where it wills; you hear the sound thereof but cannot tell whence it comes nor whither it goes. So is every one in his soul. So is every one who comes into the consciousness of himself as a son of God. When you touch that consciousness, you touch the universe. When you touch that consciousness, you touch eternal life. When you touch that consciousness, you touch God, you touch Christ, you touch all that is holy and pure and good and everlasting.

Strange. We know these things when we sit down and think them carefully through. It is because we live so superficially from day to day, it is because we refuse to dare the inward vastness of our souls, that we are like strangers in a strange land. Listen to Jesus telling the story of the mysterious adventure of our outer into our inner consciousness. Let me paraphrase it:

A certain man had two sons, an outer and an inner consciousness. And the outer consciousness said, "Give me my inheritance. Give me my world, my visible, lovely glittering world. Give me my human tastes and appetites, my desire for what I can touch and smell and taste and see."

And the inheritance was given him. There is the mystery of the incarnation, why the soul comes into form and matter and time and space.

The prodigal son played with his outwardness for a long while. Then one day he discovered that outwardness did not satisfy him. He had all he could eat and drink. He had all the enjoyments that were so necessary to him. Then he made the discovery that the things he thought were valuable were like the husks that feed the swine. They were not enough. And he began to be in want. Then suddenly he came to himself.

That is the secret. He came to himself. He found that the real joy was in himself.

In the play *They Knew What They Wanted* the tramp boasts about the good time he has with his body. The old kindly understanding priest listens and smiles, and then with his lovely Irish voice answers, "Yes, you have a good time with your body, my son. But let me tell you I have much more fun with my soul than you have with your body."

You will find that you can have more fun with your soul than you can have with your body. That discovery comes when you find Jesus of Nazareth in yourself. It was because Paul was so true to that inward self that in after-years he wrote: God was in Jesus. God in Jesus reconciled the world to Himself. Now God is in me. I find that when God is in me, my world becomes reconciled. It is no longer my enemy. It becomes my friend. It gives me all the wealth of the everlasting. I rise up on the wings of my newly discovered soul and find myself, through that upward flight, in the presence of the Eternal.

IV

GOD BECOMES MAN

UNTIL we abandon the habit of personalizing Christ, we shall never discover the inner mystery of the Christ principle working in ourselves. Jesus described it as yeast hid in the lump until the whole is leavened. The Christ principle is the love of God become man. Man is God's vehicle of revelation. Through our common humanity the manifestation of divine sonship is happening on this planet. It happened not only in Jesus. It happened in Buddha, in Confucius, in Laotze, in Moses, in Orpheus.

Traditional Christianity lost the secret long ago, and yet it has always been here from the beginning of civilization. St. Paul's point of conversion was when it dawned upon him that Jesus, the Galilean Carpenter, contained it so completely that anybody who resisted the man resisted the principle; and so he united the two. The difficulty of Christianity has been in separating Jesus of Nazareth from the universal incarnating principle which we call Christ. We

do well to follow Jesus, loyally and wholeheartedly, as the apostle did, because in him dwelt
that fulness. As we follow him, we develop and
reveal the fulness in ourselves.

Let us turn for a moment to a well-thumbed
passage in the Epistle to the Ephesians:

"For this reason, then, I kneel before the Father
from whom every family in heaven and on earth de-
rives its name and nature, praying Him out of the
wealth of his glory to grant you a mighty increase of
strength by his Spirit in the inner man."

We derive our name and nature from God. As
long as we think that God is alien to ourselves,
our prayers fall to the ground. That is the reason why so many people have stopped praying.
The science of prayer is in the recognition of
this indwelling Christ principle as something
that is the real man. We are unreal until we
have found that principle in ourselves.

The inner man is the container of the Christ
principle. That inner man has always lived. He
is beyond time and space. When we talk of immortality or the survival of the soul after death,
we mock the inner man. Death cannot touch
him. Death cannot touch God. Sin cannot touch

God. There is something in us that death and sin cannot touch. Sin and death can enter only into the outer courts of our human being. The sin of which we are guilty is in deliberately dwelling in those outer courts, in refusing to pass through the veil into the sanctuary. The suffering in the world is derived from the fact that man is not yet prepared to enter into the Holy of Holies.

When Jesus said, "Blessed are the pure in heart for they shall see God," he meant: Blessed are the people whose faith is established, whose knowledge is so sound that they walk perpetually in the presence of God. The pure in heart are they whose faith is undivided, simple, and direct. Faith is no blind fumbling of a soul. Faith is that certain touch on reality which the soul has gained by its experience with its indwelling power. As a tight-rope walker learns automatically to keep his balance, a soul, by trying again and again, learns automatically to stand at ease before the Infinite.

One of the certain signs of the Christ principle is kindness. Even if we knew nothing about the mystery of this Christ principle save its manifestation through our tendency to be kind, we should know enough to work it through; and as we work it through, we discover that it is more than kindness. It becomes at last love crucified. It becomes love completely impersonal and detached. It becomes a love that no longer seeks its own, a love that is humility, a love that is a suffering servant, a love that is as high and as wonderful as the Galilean's.

Waste no time in dreaming and going into ecstasies about the Carpenter of Nazareth. Why should you, when you and he meet in this Christ principle? Before the foundations of the earth were laid, the Christ in your inner man and the Christ in the inner man of Jesus were among the morning stars that sang together, the sons of God who shouted for joy. We have always lived in eternity. Somewhere we entered into time and space. The opposites of God are limitations, and the only limitations of which the soul has any consciousness are these limitations of time and space. When the apocalyptic seer wrote of the ultimate attainment of the soul of man, he said, "There shall be no more sea," no more separation.

Do not seek, therefore, to bridge the seeming gulf between your soul and the soul of your loved one who has gone from his body. You cannot build a bridge by the séance method. There is a higher way than that. It is the way of Jesus. It is the way of accepting common humanity and demonstrating our Christhood, though we do it alone. If Jesus did it, we must do it. We must not waste our time in sentimental talk about the beauty of Jesus. We must make our beauty like the beauty of Jesus. We must make our world like his world. The people who met him are meeting us at every point. We must not be satisfied with Jesus. We must be Jesus in ourselves.

That is what Paul meant: May Christ dwell in your hearts as you have faith, as you have discovered that you are being resurrected into that principle from moment to moment. May you be so fixed and founded in love.

Love must be broad. Most of us are narrow in our loving. What is the breadth of your love? How much does it include? Does it rule anybody out? The point where you rule anybody out is where you shut the door on your Christhood.

There can be no excuse; if you would have your full-orbed Christhood, nobody must interfere with it. Sacrifice your prejudices, your angers, your memories. Let them go, and walk in the fulness of the redeemed.

What is the length of your loving? Does it go into your yesterdays? Does it step fearlessly out into your tomorrows? In order that love should be long, there must be no worry, no uncertainty. Your consciousness must overflow all the barriers of yesterday and of today. There must be no empty regrets. Jesus said: The man who puts his hand to the plough and looks back, is not fit for the kingdom of God. You will drive your furrow crookedly if you spend too much time looking over your yesterdays. Your yesterdays are no measure of you. You are timeless. Dismiss the beautiful memories, or the ugly memories, of the past. If you look upon them at all, look upon them from the height of your conscious Christhood. They will live there, and there only will they live in beauty. Look at them from no outer place of your human, physical consciousness. Stop holding on to your past. Go forth into the length of your love. I say to people who mourn: Remember, in wasting tears on your dead, you are neglecting living people. They do not want your tears. They want your smiles, your comfort. The world is full of lonely and unhappy people. Why are you adding to its loneliness and unhappiness? Why do you stand weeping at the tomb? Love must be long, as it must be broad and inclusive.

But love must be more than length and more than breadth. Love must be depth. Are there any deeps of human experience from which you shrink? Do you ever hide your head from the tragedies of people? Is your love afraid to plumb the depth of poverty, of sorrow? The cross of Christ went through all the sorrow and the poverty and the anguish of the world. It went through the heart of hell itself and came out on the other side, until its depth became a height. Let your height and depth become one thing—the soul's perpendicular in the presence of love unbounded and unconditioned.

Theologians are fond of saying that "in Jesus dwelt all the fulness of the Godhead bodily." We grant it—in Jesus dwelt all the fulness of the Godhead bodily. But St. Paul would say,

[246]

That is not enough. You must have the same fulness of the Godhead in your body.

I discover that conventional Christians are always talking about the divinity of Jesus, the deity of Jesus. Of course he was God. But why are you not also God? Of course he was divine. But what is wrong with your divinity? Why do you rest satisfied with the achievement of one man's divinity? Go on achieving in your own right. Surely the cross means that. So the world, when it touches you, will come at last to say with Thomas, "My Lord and my God." No life can be a redeeming life until it has, in a measure, experienced that.

Until the name of Jesus and your name blend into one beauty, you will not have found that resurrection which awaits you when you have been properly crucified. Bless you in your crucifixion, and bless you in that ultimate, certain resurrection as you go upon love's appointed way.

II

St. Paul offered to his world the only kind of evidence a soul can offer while it is still in a physical body—the evidence of courage and of strength, of patience and of gladness. His language was the language of one humbled by the glory of an experience that had changed him from one kind to another kind of man.

Some of these sayings may sound as though they were only words. They will sound like that if God is an enigma, if life on this planet blurs the vision so that one cannot see God face to face. Why should life on this planet blur the vision of God? The answer is, Because God does not seem to "work." Men of thought have ruled Him out. They see no evidence for the existence of God, in a universe like ours. Astronomers have hunted for God with a telescope, and all they have found is a series of universes. Men of the laboratory have investigated the composition and structure of matter and have concluded that it is nothing but a chemical accident. Psychologists have peered into the mystery of the human soul and have replied, "Only complexes."

What, then, led Jesus to the illusion of believing that he and God were one? And was St. Paul—so sure of God, so sure of the indwelling Christ, believing that the bond between him and Jesus was an inner experience called Christ

[248]

—under the spell of phantasy? Are we to rule out these witnesses and prefer the evidence of the men of science and of psychology, who have written their *Yea* to their own theory and their *Nay* to the theory of Jesus and of Paul?

This can only be met by what we ourselves have found through living on this planet. What was it that Paul found? Here is a record of his discovery: "I appeal to you as a worker with God." He could appeal only to people who believed that they and God worked together, that God is a co-operative force in human history; that God is something more than a chemical accident or a blind tendency; that God is something in the universe that becomes man, and that man is something in the universe that becomes God. Is that flimsy thinking? Our answer will be determined by our experience.

"God is love," wrote a great mystic, out of the full experience of his life with Christ, "and every one who loves is born of God and knows God." The knowledge is attained not by thinking but by feeling. If you ask an artist what is the secret of his art, he will not tell you it is his technique. He will describe his technique as a skill that has come to him through his constancy and devotion to what he calls beauty: through his repeated efforts to incarnate what he calls beauty in the form of his art, he has acquired an ease of expression. But he will not tell you that his technique is his art. He will say, "No, my art is my love of beauty. It is my belief in beauty. It is my awareness of beauty as the very soul of this material universe. I find beauty everywhere."

If you ask the saint what path led him into the presence of God, he will answer, "The path began in my heart. When I discovered that my interests in life were not devoted solely to the contemplation of myself and my needs, my aches and my pains, or my joys and my gladnesses; when I discovered that I was going out more and more to people, that I found in men and women and children something that satisfied me, the fact of God became a reality. It was as I felt toward people, it was as my joy in people was greater than my indifference to people or my contempt of them, that God at last became real. I was a partner with that in the universe which wells up in me as love."

Religion is logical, in spite of those moments when it seems to break down all the methods of argument. What is logic? Logic is to the thinker what technique is to the artist. The thinker knows his logic is only the technique of his thinking. It is the form through which he communicates what he knows. He knows that what he knows is more than the technique of his knowledge. So the true logician is never confined to his technique, any more than a great artist is confined to his technique. The genius always breaks down the method of his expression, revealing that, in spite of his skill, his knowledge transcends his skill and sometimes leads him to set aside the old skill because he finds it no longer adequate.

This also happens in religion. That is why we break through our technique—theology, the symbols of our religion. But we are not to suppose that in this freedom of the soul to find new expressions of its discoveries, there is anything destructive or iconoclastic. We have already touched upon the story of Moses coming down from the mountain. He had been talking face to face with God as a man talks to a friend, to discover that his brother and the group he had left behind had made a god out of their earrings and their rings and their bangles. It was natural. We find the unknown through the known, and the man who has climbed the hill of his soul will no longer be satisfied with the concepts which once satisfied him.

But Moses was not very kind. He broke the god and made the people drink the dust thereof, to prove the futility of their childish concept. We must not forget that Jesus emptied a temple and denounced those who were buying and selling and trafficking in a holy place. Moments are inevitable in the growth of the soul when the indwelling Christ sternly drives forth from the mind inadequate and no longer tenable ideas of God.

Can we blame a man for seeking to remove from the thought of people trinket-concepts of the universe, when he has found that all that we mean by God is gathered up in the soul and that people cannot be emancipated from their slavery to old superstitions while they continue to fashion God out of their playthings? We may allow a child for a time to have his toys, but the time comes when, out of very loyalty, we must take them away and say, "You are no longer a child. You are beginning to grow up. Behold your God."

We sing, in one of the best of hymns:

> "New mercies each returning day,
> Hover around us while we pray;
> New perils past, new sins forgiven,
> New thoughts of God, new hopes of heaven."

Jesus was a man with new thoughts of God, with new hopes of heaven. St. Paul was a man with new thoughts of God, with new hopes of heaven. This is an age with new thoughts of God and new hopes of heaven, and it must at times be stern in saying to us, "You must leave the nursery and go forth to study. You must face yourself in your dignity as a son. While you were a child, it was right for you to behave as a child. But this age is not an age of childhood. It is an age of grown-up-ness. Here is a new thought of God, a new thought of Christ. Here is a new thought of religion, a new thought of the universe. Let us be squared with the newness of that thought and the freshness of that hope."

[253]

If we could only bear witness of our conscious Christhood to this world, how the world would be changed! We have been experimenting of late with statutes and with leagues, but they do not save the world. Mankind will always be mankind, tied up with war and vice and crime, until man begins to take up his residence in the dignity of his own clearly visioned Christhood. So long as we make Christ objective, some one outside ourselves, we shall never be successful. But when the moment comes that the Christ in us is active and we join the group of those in whom the same Christ is active, then the world will go forward—and not until then.

The inspiration and example of Jesus must give us courage to stand up to the disciplines of our own life. We cannot escape those disciplines. They are initiations into our Christhood; and, if we dodge them, we shall never find that Christhood. We must endure hardness as good soldiers, for the Christ that is in us. We must ask for no exceptions. When we discover ourselves stripped bare of all the things we once held precious, we shall find a new preciousness resident in our nature.

"O Corinthians!" What passion of loving is in those words—what brotherhood in them, too. "I am keeping nothing back from you. My heart is wide open for you," that you may find this thing, that you may be set free, that you may walk in the light of your soul's resurrection.

III

If we would practise our Christhood, we must begin to be aware of the inner communion and fellowship of a high experience. It is not easy to serve God and Mammon. It is not easy to be our true self if we are still centred in the outer courts of our consciousness. We have no longer a place in the world of outwardness. We must make no compromise. We have been frustrated and weakened by our social passions, ardors, ambitions. So many people discover that it is difficult for them to practise the companionship of Christ in the group to which they long ago gave themselves. When they come to me, my answer always is: Sunder yourself. You no longer belong to that group. Find yourself in the heart of the host that is waiting for you. You are compassed about with a cloud of witnesses. Go into them, and when you go into them, you have only one standard of companionship—experience: "Do I see in this person the constraining love of what I know to be Christ? Are these people swayed by the ardors and the compassion of the Christ consciousness? Then I belong to them."

That is the reason why Christianity made such rapid progress in the first and second centuries. After that, it dwindled because the disciples began making compromises with the world of the outward order. We chain a ball to our legs if we continue to make compromises with these people.

As we grow older in the companionship of an inward experience, our strength and our consistency grow in proportion to our loyalty to that one communion and fellowship. We find that the people outside do not understand us. We recall the story of Orpheus, who came down from God out of heaven to bring beauty into the world. He sought to give the world beauty. He went hither and yon among the people of the carnal mind, and suddenly they turned on him and tore him to pieces.

There is a lament and a regret in the words of the Fourth Gospel, concerning the coming of Jesus: "He came unto his own, and his own received him not." When he came into the outer courts of human consciousness, they rejected and crucified him. But when he came into the inner courts, he found the sons of God waiting for him. "As many as received him, to them gave he power to become the sons of God." All the time that we can give to humanity must be consumed in our devotion to the communion and the fellowship. I am not talking about church-Christianity. I am talking about the saints—about people of tenderness and compassion. Why should we not open our hearts to them, since they have opened their hearts to us? Why should we dawdle in the outer courts among "the lesser breed without the law"?

Begin cultivating the communion and the fellowship. All about you are these shining ambassadors of Christ. Take up your residence not only in the inner courts of your divine consciousness, but in the inner courts of the divine consciousness of this planet. Belong to the real aristocracy—the aristocracy of the lovers—and not to the bourgeoisie of the haters and the sneerers. Leave them alone, unless they meet you on your terms. If you see them coming up in response to you, meet them and lift them up. But make no compromise with the kind of people you used to know. You will be hampered and hindered by them. Swing out and swing free into this new fellowship. Great adventures await you. Loves you have never known will shine upon you like the stars in the heavens. Beautiful voices will take up the song celestial and on every side you will be touched by the lonely lord Christs who have waited over-long for your companionship.

Look out upon your world today and watch the shining multitude under the white banner of Christ—people of tenderness and of compassion. Ask of them no labels and no signs. There is only one label—Christ; and only one sign— his wounded heart, his hands, his feet, and his head. But when you see those signs, you will know you have found a companion. Be at one in that companionship. No longer prostitute your Christhood by the old compromises.

To St. Paul a believer was one who was under

the constraint of love, and an unbeliever was one who doubted the constraining power of love. The unbeliever and the infidel is the hater, the despiser, the scorner, the mocker.

This glorious bit from the ninety-first Psalm has all Christianity contained within its stanzas:

"Whoso dwelleth under the defence of the Most High, shall abide under the shadow of the Almighty"—

You will no longer be afraid of the old terrors that used to come by night—the arrows of gossip and slander; of the pestilence of suspicion and of hatred that used to walk in the darkness of your soul; of the sickness that used to destroy you in the noonday.

"A thousand shall fall beside thee, and ten thousand at thy right hand; but it shall not come nigh thee.
"Yea, with thine eyes shalt thou behold; and see the reward of the ungodly."

The ungodly are those who live in the midst of these terrors, who are poisoned by these dreadful arrows they carry in the quivers on their own backs. They shoot them continually, but the same arrows come back to them, and they are in perpetual agony.

Of late there have been many suicides of outstanding men. Why do people commit suicide? Some may say, "Because of insanity." But why should a mind go insane? Because it refuses its Godhood and asserts its beastliness. If you dwell in the outer courts all the time, you will go insane. But if you come under the shadow of God, you will be sane. There will be no more of the sting of the arrow that drives so many people to self-destruction. The self-pity of people, the loneliness of souls who have ruled God out, ends ultimately in the denial of the worth-whileness of life, and so they destroy their bodies.

It is not my business now to discuss what happens to people who step out of their bodies after destroying them. There is much matter in that, but it does not belong in these discussions. But it does fit into the fact that, in the understanding of the mystery of incarnation, souls are in bodies for education. When a soul destroys its body, it becomes a truant. It is the expression of a disobedient son who will not accept his disciplines and his lessons. The reason why we need to live in the communion and the fellowship is because we thereby derive a better understanding of life itself and a deepening faith in its meaning.

"Walk with the godly." I do not mean godliness in the sense of what appears to be pious or conventional. The godly man is a lover. God is love, and in proportion to the degree of the love-power of our hearts do we hold the consciousness of God. There is no other way to hold that consciousness. We must renounce the life of hate. We must practise the discipline of love. There is a cross, with its thorns and nails, in the discipline. Our lives will supply us from day to day with all those disciplines. Overcome that cranky aunt or that impossible uncle. Learn to be gentle with the over-demanding mother or the tyrannical father, with the foolish brother or the selfish sister. We must set our kindness and our faith against all the scorn and the mockery that we find in the world today.

But when we need strength, when we are tired of out-post duty, we can enter into the courts of the companionship of the comrades of Jesus. That is why Paul said, "Be separate." Begin to set yourself free from these scoffing and abandoned ones. In their presence we cannot always practise the fulness of our Christ consciousness. It is well for us occasionally to listen to him who said, "Evil communications corrupt good manners. Awake to righteousness, and sin not; for some have not the knowledge of God. I speak this to your shame."

If you are in earnest concerning the way of the Christ, if you want the way, make your decision now. And let this be the decision: I will enter into the waiting communion and fellowship of the conscious Christs of my age. I will walk with them and work with them, suffer with them, and die for them. Enter the aristocracy of Christs. Turn your back upon Belial and his host. Make no more compromises. Come out and walk in the glory of this new day of the companionship of Jesus.

> Companion of the highroad, hail! all hail!
> Day on his shoulder flame of sunset bears,
> As he goes marching where the autumn flares
> A banner to the sky; in russet mail
> The trees are trooping hither to assail
> Twilight with spears; a rank of coward cares
> Creep up, as though to take us unawares,
> And find their stratagems of none avail.

GOD BECOMES MAN

Accept the challenge of the royal hills,
And dare adventure as we always dared!
Life with red wine his golden chalice fills,
And bids us drink to all who forward fared—
Those lost, white armies of the host of dream;
Those dauntless, singing pilgrims of the Gleam!*

* *His Lady of the Sonnets*, McClelland and Stewart.

V

TEMPLES OF THE LIVING GOD

WE have been so accustomed to think of God as a power outside and beyond ourselves, instead of thinking of Him as a power within and belonging to ourselves, that it is not easy to separate our thinking from that tradition which through the ages has held men and women together in their desire to behold the King in his beauty. Because we have been meditating upon the mystery of the indwelling or incarnating God, it now seems time for us to reach a definite and clear conclusion of the whole matter concerning the fellowship and the communion of the saints.

How are we to interpret St. Paul's statement: "We are the temple of the living God"? How can man be the temple of God unless God has already taken up His habitation in man? When did God take up that habitation? There we touch the mystery which baffles us, not because of the darkness in it but because of the superabundance of light. We are dazzled by the splendor of the possibility of this truth concerning ourselves, that somehow God and man are eternally one. They always have been one, they always will be. But men and women do not always know it, and out of that ignorance comes what we call sin—missing the mark, the reason for our incarnation. We waste our divine energies by clouding that inner force and radiance through our insistence upon the outer consciousness as the only consciousness.

As we look into our lives, we discover there our difficulty. It is so easy to dwell only in the body, to submit to the tyranny of physical sensation and desire. There is nothing essentially wrong in sensation and in desire. The wrong begins when physical sensation and desire dominate our consciousness. Until we have conquered that tyranny, we live in a state of sin. We are only released from that sin when we look into ourselves, in obedience to the law which Jesus declared: Enter into yourself. You never pray outside yourself. You may think you do, but your words fall to the ground. All our outward acts of devotion, of words, and of deeds are valueless unless they are consciously guided from within.

If we desert the indwelling God to prostrate ourselves before an out-dwelling God, we deny the real God. That sounds as though we ruled out God transcendent, in order to hold God immanent or indwelling. We do not; we include them both. But we are proceeding from the witness of holy men and women, that only as they found themselves in the unity of their Godhood by discovering that innately God dwelt in them, did they find God in His surpassing splendor and beauty. A prayer to God that does not proceed from the fact that we, too, are in the nature of Godhood, is of no value.

If I said this on my own authority, it would be impertinent as well as dangerous; but it is what Jesus said. It is what the New Testament reiterates. It is stated by St. Paul: "We are the temple of God." The real Church is your self. The holiest of sanctuaries is your self, not your outer self, not your self as related to a visible body, but your self as related to the mystery of an eternal and invisible soul.

[266]

One of the abiding heresies of our time is derived from the teaching of the Behaviorists and their school, as well as of the Freudians and their school, who teach that the soul is only a bundle of habits, that we can change the habits by developing new and better ones. But do we change the fact that all that is meant by the soul is a bundle of habits? If that were true, life would have no meaning. If we think of ourselves as a bundle of pious habits, including church-going and sacrament-taking, godly deeds with a polite and dignified demeanor, we insult and deny the source of our power. The deed that we do has no value unless it is an extension of our real self.

Some of you may ask, "But how can we find that self?" Tennyson, in his prefece to *In Memoriam*, wrote what I think is a sensible description of the way to that discovery:

"Strong Son of God, Immortal Love,
    Whom we that have not seen Thy face,
    By faith and faith alone embrace,
    Believing where we cannot prove."

Before we analyze that statement, remember that faith is experience. We must clear our minds concerning that precious word. I seek to uproot from your minds the fallacy that faith has anything to do with a blind mental or spiritual obedience to an authoritative statement or personality beyond ourselves. Faith is in us, our knowledge of a power that we have tried—and we have discovered that the power not only works but that it works beneficially. It is an experience of an inner divine power that is unconquerable if we give it a chance.

Love, in its lower aspects, is related to physical emotion and desire. But if we limit it to a physical emotion and desire, we discover that love is an uncertain power. A young man once came to me to tell of his problem in discovering God—how he had thought his way through concepts which to him were no longer adequate, and had found that love was God. But love to him was a young woman, lovely, charming, ineffably dear. Then something happened. Love ceased to be for him authoritative. It had gone wrong. I met the difficulty by leading him from the outer to the inner courts of his consciousness; I said to him, "If love be rightly love, you still love. What made you love her? Did you love

[268]

her for what was outward and visible? Was not your love a recognition of something infinitely beautiful and good within the lady of your choice?" He admitted it.

"Well," I added, "you still love the infinitely good and the beautiful. Take now your love, which seems to have been frustrated, and conduct it into this inner court of divine consciousness, and you will hold it forever."

If we take this interpretation, in harmony with the thirteenth chapter of the First Epistle to the Corinthians, we have no difficulty in discovering that this is what St. Paul meant by his experience with that One whom Tennyson named Strong Son of God, Immortal Love— a love that does not die, that goes on whether it has been betrayed by a kiss or deserted by an act of cowardice. It still goes on in its divine gesture, including all its original objects. Paul named this immortal love charity, *caritas*. As he recalled what had happened to him since he met Jesus on the road to Damascus, he discovered that the historic Galilean Carpenter had carried him into himself; that his devotion to Jesus had evoked from himself a quality that

was the same quality which he found in Jesus,
and so he wrote:

"I may speak with the tongues of men and of angels,
     but if I have no love,
I am a noisy gong or a clanging cymbal.
I may prophesy, fathom all mysteries and secret lore,
I may have such absolute faith that I can move hills
     from their place,
but if I have no love, I count for nothing;
I may distribute all I possess in charity,
I may give up my body to be burnt,
but if I have no love, I make nothing of it."

It makes no difference what your practices
may have been, however pious and however
good, unless they are consciously directed by
the indwelling principle of love, they become
as a sounding brass and a tinkling cymbal.
Your devotion to the Church is dust; even the
outward integrity and morality of your life,
your conformity to traditions and standards,
mean nothing. It is better to be outwardly rebellious and to be governed by that inward principle, than to be outwardly conformed and to
be divorced from that indwelling flame and
principle of beauty.

Following Jesus is not easy. By his own statement, he has described it as hard: If any of you will follow after me, remember there is a cross involved. It is not mine, good friend, it is your own. A bitter discipline, a terrible anguish, is involved, if you take this way of initiation into the mystery of the kingdom of God. Then toward the end, as though to reassure and comfort them, he said: But do not be discouraged. I have taught you how to overcome the world.

When he said, "I have overcome the world," he did not mean vicariously. One of the perils of our theological thinking is in assuming that Jesus has done everything for us. He has done everything for us in this sense only: demonstrating by his life the principles of the law of our Christhood. If we take him as a Master and follow him faithfully, in leading ourselves up into his life, we shall have no difficulty except that of enduring the inevitable disciplines necessary to the attainment of our conscious Christhood.

You remember the two young men who came to him and said, "We would like to have your power." What they meant was: May we, when your kingdom is established, have two special thrones of authority? Let one of us have the right hand and the other the left. And Jesus answered: "But that is not mine to give." He meant, It is not mine to give; but it is yours to attain! If you want it, you must be prepared for the initiations. Are you willing to go all the way with me? Are you ready, are you able, to drink of the cup that I drink and to be baptized with the baptism I am baptized with? That is the way he has been speaking to his disciples ever since. That is how he is speaking to us to-day.

Do not think that I make light of the sacraments. I believe in them; I practise them; I have joy in them. Do not think that I make light of the Church. It has given me all I know and have. I can say of the Church, "If I forget thee, O Jerusalem, let my right hand forget her cunning." Nobody in all the world of Christendom so needs the companionship of the communion and fellowship called the Church as I. But when I remember how, for a long while, I saw it only in its outwardness, and it gave me nothing but despair and defeat; when I realize how people are missing the inward mystery by putting the emphasis upon the objectivities of the sacramental, the sacerdotal, and the ecclesiastical systems, I must sound a note of warning—the note that Jesus gave to his disciples: "Not every one that saith unto me, Lord, Lord, shall enter into the kingdom of heaven; but he that doeth the will of my Father which is in heaven."

In the garden of Gethsemane it was hard for him to do God's will. The story is told in a simple, beautiful, brief way, but behind the brevity and the simplicity and the beauty I feel hours of loneliness—the shudder, the agony, the passion, the sweat, as of a young athlete, and then the complaining and the pleading from the outer courts of his consciousness: Save me from drinking it! This was the cup of which he had spoken to the sons of Zebedee, and yet he himself was trying to escape it: Oh, if it be possible, can I not get into this knowledge without this suffering, without this sorrow, without this loneliness? How can I find the way into my Christhood apart from a world like this?

But there is no way apart from a world like this. It must be dared and endured to the end.

You ask me, "How can I find the way into

this consciousness of a son of God?" I answer: Begin your life as though you were living on earth for the first time. Forget all your failures, your wanderings, and your complainings. Begin now to be brave. Exercise your hardihood. Practise the presence of Christ in your daily and hourly consciousness. Practise loving as you have never practised it before, and you will discover that the former practice was only self-loving. You loved those who loved you. You responded to those who were kind to you. Learn to say, as for the first time, "Forgive us our trespasses, as we forgive those who trespass against us." For the Christhood which is being resurrected in us, we thank thee, thou great demonstrator of the indwelling Christ——the human soul——for the wonder of it, for the breathless adventure of it, for the amazing beauty of it, for the royal worth of it. We now begin, by our experience, to say with St. Paul: My body is God's Church. My body is God's holy Mass, Eucharist, sacrament. My body is the abiding place of my Lord.

II

All who have the force which we call experience are summoned to organize it into social action. Once that experience has been enjoyed, the next step is the organization of those who share it into social redemption. The discovery of our inward Christness leads us to do the thing which Jesus did when he was with us in the days of his flesh.

As St. Paul looked back over the life of Jesus, he was impressed by the mystery of its graciousness. He realized that Jesus stood for this fact, that a soul in a body is a manifestation of an utter giving. We are here because we have given ourselves or we had never been born. We do not come accidentally into the world. We come, as we have already found, on secret service, under sealed orders, and we do not realize ourselves until we open the document, read it, and follow its instructions.

We cannot open the document unless we enter into communion with our high selfhood. We must practise our love, however attenuated it may be at first. We must dare our kindness, however evanescent. We must judge ourselves by our moments of *unconscious* kindness, until we have made them conscious. How wonderful we are when we release the power of our kindness, and how ordinary we are when we dam it up. Jesus said—and every saint knows it is true— "Whatsoever thou shalt bind on earth shall be bound in heaven; and whatsoever thou shalt loose on earth shall be loosed in heaven." Heaven is dependent upon our consciousness and upon our deed. The whole universe is quivering and on tiptoe to be set free through our conscious act and our conscious thought. When we have come to that we shall understand the rest of the mystery. But we shall never understand it until we have begun to practise our Godhood, our Christhood.

You have found yourself, Paul said, in God. The world is a troubled world, a baffled world. What will you do about it? If the saviour in Jesus saved you by helping you to release your Godhood, you are bound to help the world by helping somebody else release his Godhood. How did Jesus save you by helping you to release your Godhood? By making you realize, through the quality of his life, Godhood in a man.

The centuries of Christian thinking have covered up the original ecstasy of the discovery of such a force as a common Christhood among the believers. It has ended in our separating Jesus' Christhood from our Christhood. We have set him on a pinnacle. We have placed him over an altar. We have burned candles and incense before him, but we have never thought of burning candles and incense before the enthroned consciousness which is Christ in ourselves, manifesting itself through our kindness. Because of this difficulty, we need to read a saying from another letter, written to the Philippians. It is the heart of the gospel, and it is what I mean when I speak of organizing our Christ consciousness into social redemption:

"By every incentive of love, by all your participation in the Spirit, by all your affectionate tenderness, I pray you to give me the utter joy of knowing you are living in harmony, with the same feelings of love, with one heart and soul, never acting for private ends or from vanity, but humbly considering each other the better man, and each with an eye to the interests of others as well as to his own. Treat one another with the same spirit as you experience in Christ Jesus."

[277]

If I do not salute the Christ in you, my saluting the Christ in Jesus is an empty act. My adoration of Jesus is dust unless I give you equal adoration. Until I have learned to salute you in your Christness and as a son of God, I insult Jesus.

We have described faith as experience, the working power of the Christ consciousness, which we find to be the fundamental force of our personality. By experience we know that, though at times we are malicious, cruel, and empty in our pursuits, we are real as we release tenderness and kindness. We are disintegrated when we are away from that enthroned consciousness. But how organized and powerful when we are saluting our Christ on his throne in our consciousness!

"Though he was divine by nature, he did not snatch at equality with God but emptied himself by taking the nature of a servant; born in human guise and appearing in human form, he humbly stooped in his obedience even to die, and to die upon the cross. Therefore God raised him high and conferred on him a Name above all names, so that before the Name of Jesus every knee should bend in heaven, on earth, and underneath the earth, and every tongue confess that 'Jesus Christ is Lord,' to the glory of God the Father."

[278]

He did not regard even Godhood or the heaven world so much. He thought the adventure of incarnation was the highest adventure of a son of God, and he came deliberately into self-limitation. I argue: So do we. I argue and insist: So have we. And until we know that, we shall never discover ourselves. But when we find it, what power is released, as it was released in Jesus!

If you still insist that Jesus is separate in nature from the rest of mankind, that he must be adored as the second Person in the holy Trinity, there is an answer in a statement from the writer of the Epistle to the Hebrews. To me it is one of the most amazing writings in the New Testament. I would advise you either to write it out and keep it in your room, to look at when you are dressing and undressing, or to learn it by heart and master it:

"In bringing many sons to glory, it was befitting that He [God] for whom and by whom the universe exists, should perfect the Pioneer of their salvation by suffering. For sanctifier and sanctified have all one origin."

We cannot get away from that. If we bring our quaint mediæval theology against that, we are defeated. We must no longer separate the divinity of Jesus from our divinity, his Christhood from our Christhood, his sonship from our sonship. Read through Paul's epistles and watch him storming at the people who refused to grasp what he knew was the real power of the gospel, the manifestation of divine sonship.

Paul understood the principle of evolution better than we suspect. It was not Darwin who discovered it. Paul knew all about it when he wrote in the Epistle to the Romans: The whole creation groans and travails together until now for one object—the manifestation of the sons of God. The eons of time in which this planet was forming from the fire-mist, the jelly-fish and the saurian, the crystal and the cell, had only one object—man's hour of divine manifestation. The urge of evolution was completed when Jesus came in our manhood and demonstrated that man is the only begotten son of God. Then began a new history for man on this planet. He began to take up his divine inheritance. So Paul wrote, in that same Epistle:

"There is therefore now no condemnation to them which are in Christ Jesus, who walk not after the flesh but after the Spirit,

"For the law of the Spirit of life in Christ Jesus hath made me free from the law of sin and death."

When we have discovered the Christ in ourselves, we are no longer enslaved. We may walk for a long while with the lock-step of the old slavery, but by gradual degrees we shall assume the rhythm and the dignity of our Christhood. We may for a long while show the scars of the shackles that were once on our wrists and on our ankles, but by degrees those scars will become glorified.

That is what happens every time a son of God is changed from his physical to his spiritual consciousness. How the scars of the former state of our deliberately chosen thraldom begin to have a luster as of the sky! There is no beauty on earth equivalent to the beauty of a soul redeemed into its consciousness, and aligned with Jesus in redeeming people from the fetters of fear and of suspicion, of jealousy and of envy, of hatred and of malice.

A lyric from my friend and companion, Kenneth Leslie, bears out what I have been saying and describes in Jesus the movement of his release. He was not always free. He made himself free. We have not always been free. We must make ourselves free, by trusting our kindness. It will lead us further into the throne room of our Christhood.

"One had whispered: 'Be at peace!
Nothing can assail
This glad hymn of wood to wood
Wedded with a nail.'

One had taught his skilful hand
All his heart's desire,
Edged his saw with husky song,
His plane with running fire.

Now that same One touched him
While his foot-lathe droned.
Hinted at a question
He had long postponed.

Pushed him from his doorway
And his present task,
Burned him with the question
He had dared to ask,

Till the bannered morning
And the trumps of noon,
Dreadful drums of sunset,
Ghost pipes of the moon,

Blew their woeful challenge,
Shook their mad dismay,
Beat their fearful summons;
And he could not stay.

[282]

Cattle-yoke forgotten,
Shavings in his hair,
Queer dream choking him,
Dream that he must dare:

Thus he took the open road,
He and his good Friend,
Ready for its dalliance
And its bitter end."

Our good Friend is God the Father. We must no longer dally with the denial of our sonship. We must leave the lathe and the saw and the work-bench. We must shake our heads free of the shavings and the accumulations of the work hour. Forth now into our world, mobbed and ready against us, ready to crucify us. We must set the power of our love, of our kindness, and of our gentleness, against the children of the outer darkness, until we redeem them—though we die in that redemption.

III

St. Paul was always careful to distinguish between his personality and his selfhood, between his outwardness and his inwardness. He emphasized this distinction so well that tradition misunderstood him and pictured St. Paul as a kind of misshapen dwarf, when probably he was splendid in his physical manifestation. He wanted people to find the real indwelling Christ who was writing those letters, who was preaching those sermons, who was healing the sick, giving sight to the blind, and causing the lame to walk. He wanted to lead people into their own inner splendor, and so he ridiculed the outward. We must not listen to theologians who try to prove that St. Paul was bow-legged, hook-nosed, and unpleasing. The fact that he was once taken for Hermes, the most handsome of the gods, proves the contrary. Physically he must have been outwardly appealing, as his Master was.

Outward appeal does not depend upon any configuration of features. We are outwardly appealing only as some inward glory in us shines through the outward. The mystery of personality is never in externals. It is an inward quality that sets one man or one woman apart from the rest of the world. We have seen handsome men and handsome women, with no more appeal or animation than dabs of clay. We have seen peo-

ple who at first had no visible beauty, but un-
expectedly the face was lighted with its own
inner magnificence.

All this is found in Paul's careful use of the
word *personality*. We must cease dwelling in the
outer courts of our physical consciousness. As
we have already seen, we go into the outer courts
to transact the Father's business. I must go
into my hands, but I do not live there. I do
my business there. I must go into my eyes—I
must go into that which is outward in order to
make my affiliation with the world of the outer
and the visible. But I can have power in that
world of the outward and the visible only when
I have entered into myself in secret, when I have
found my Father in relationship with myself as
His son, as His Lord Christ, as His most holy
Jesus, as His succession of all the saints and
the prophets and the evangelists from the beginning of man's time of incarnating upon this
planet.

"I knew a man in Christ," St. Paul wrote,
"above fourteen years ago (whether in the body,
I cannot tell; or whether out of the body, I
cannot tell; God knoweth), such an one caught

up to the third heaven. And I knew such a man (whether in the body, or out of the body, I cannot tell: God knoweth), how that he was caught up into paradise, and heard unspeakable words, which it is not lawful for a man to utter."

We have been so fond of speculating as to whether Paul actually went to paradise. Where is paradise? In the only possible place—in one's self. Where is heaven? In only one place—in one's self. But you say, "What will happen to me when I die?" I answer: Until you have died, nothing will happen. Until you have died to the slavery of dwelling only in the members of your body, you will never see God; you will never know Christ, and you will never enter into the courts of his eternal abiding.

I say this on the authority of the Master whose words we have quoted so many times: The kingdom of God comes not with observation. We cannot place it. We cannot say it is there or here. If we could only take that word of Jesus, forgetting all the rest, what power would be released in us!

We are among those who believe that the Bible is a handbook, given to the world by wise and holy men. The Christ principle is not original or new. It is as old as the love of God. In the very beginning was that Christ principle, said John, writing at the end of the first century. By that Christ principle was everything made. Nothing was made apart from it. That Christ principle became man and has dwelt among us. We have seen its glory, the glory as of the only begotten of the Father, full of grace and truth. That Christ principle is resident in our eternal selfhood. Our divine nature is its manifestation. Our body is the vehicle, through which the manifestation is given. And when we have found that, how we shall surpass the earth!

There is the story of Peter in his old age, when he had come into that consciousness: "They brought forth the sick into the streets, and laid them on beds and couches, that at least the shadow of Peter passing by might overshadow some of them." We must have that power. People must bring forth their sick when we go by. The unhappy must be made happy when they look at us or even hear the sound of our name. That is heaven, that is salvation, that is Christianity.

But, of course, we must have the mystical experience. We must know a Man. We must be able to say definitely: This week, or last week, or this summer, or last summer, or ten summers ago, I made the ascent into the Sinai of my selfhood and beheld God face to face. We shall not all get this now, though some day we shall. Why not have it now? Why go badgered and bothered by the fetterings of the old feudal system of our outer lording? We did not come on earth to make money or to be successful in our social alignments. We did not come on earth to have a pleasant time playing with our imagination and then at the end to be wafted on the wings of angels into some beautiful Valhalla of God. We have come on earth to be crucified. We have come on earth for the business of wearing a crown of thorns, to be nailed, hands and feet, upon the cross of our disciplines and to be pierced through the nature of our loving, that we may be resurrected into Christs, Redeemers, Saviours.

When we see that, we shall love life. Then for the first time we shall sing: Praise God from whom all blessings flow. Praise God for meat and drink. Praise God for companionship. Praise God for enemies. Praise God for gossips and for the clacking tongues of the unwise. Praise God for the episodic moments when I have been lifted into my heights. Praise God that out of suffering I have found my eternal selfhood.

That is to be initiated. That is to be in paradise with your soul, as St. Paul was. In his poetic way he was retelling the story of his conversion. People talk so glibly about conversion, regarding it as an acquiescence to ecclesiastical standards. Our conversion can mean only one thing: Rediscovery of ourselves in terms of what we know to be God and of what we know to be Jesus.

When I say: Trust your kindness instead of your goodness, do not think that I am laying down a gospel of hedonism or of pleasure. I am trying to say it in the sense in which I believe Jesus said it: "Except your righteousness shall exceed the righteousness of the scribes and Pharisees, ye shall in no case enter into the kingdom of heaven." There is a hard, cruel goodness. We know the cruelty of people who are always criticizing humanity, and yet outwardly their life is a conforming life. To that kind of goodness Jesus said: Depart from me, I know you not.

The Church has been hurt by a kind of traditional goodness. We have all seen people tortured by the unyielding, narrow goodness of the "unco guid." Goodness of itself is beautiful. When it comes out of the heart, it is divine. When love directs the deed, the deed will be a deed of Jesus. Love only can be the guide. Trust nothing else. Do not trust tradition or popular opinion, but trust the innate goodness of your soul. Be caught up into the third heaven of your inner self, and understand what Paul meant by the spirit, by the new birth, by conversion, and by the second Adam which is the Lord from heaven.

In his struggle to orient himself Paul found it hard to be free of the outer self. So he went to Jesus, to his Master and Teacher, saying: Jesus, help me. I want to move into the inner. I am afraid of the tyranny of the outer.

That was the thorn in his flesh. We all have thorns in the flesh, when our consciousness in the outer court of our being is over-dominant, when we dwell too much upon the outer state of our thinking and of our feeling. St. Paul said: If I could only turn from the tyranny of this outer consciousness, this animal man, I could serve you so much better.

And Jesus answered: Paul, in your very struggle to make the change, in daring the discipline of daily crucifixion, you will find growing strength. The strength of a Christ is attained by the struggle. Out of the weakness that desires strength, out of the passion and the bloody sweat, comes the strong arm of your Lord.

VI

THE CHRIST OF POWER

We are not to suppose that the way to Christhood is easy or that Christs themselves have always walked it evenly. There are bitter blows and dark moments in the soul's discovery of its Christhood—days when the human conscious mind prevails over the Christ and unconscious mind. There is a forever-war going on between the natural mind and the spiritual mind, giving us comfort to believe that, in spite of our inconsistencies and our failures, we shall yet win to the completeness of the Christ mind.

The mistake of all these centuries of Christianity has been in objectifying Christ. We must not objectify even the Holy Spirit. There is only one Holy Ghost and he resides in us. "Let this mind be in you, which was also in Christ Jesus," wrote Paul. Our mistake is in thinking that, by praying or singing, something will come down out of the sky. It does not come down out of the sky. We brought it with us when we incarnated here. It has been in us all the time, and we have not owned it. We have been afraid of it, and until we own it, accept it, and dare it, we shall pray in vain. Something in us is being crucified. Something in us has been denied and deserted, and until we accept that something in us that is Christ, we shall sing in vain to the historic companion of the long ago whom we remember by the name Jesus.

If I can only convince you of that, I shall change you; I shall send you forth with a new power. When St. Paul wrote to the Corinthians, they were beginning to separate their Christ consciousness from the Christ of Galilee and of Judea. They were beginning to elevate the objective Jesus. They were forming their theologies about him and, as a result, they were failing the thing he had come to do. When we ignore our true Christhood, our divine sonship, we begin to take up our residence in the courts of our animal consciousness. And when we take up our residence in the courts of that consciousness, this, according to St. Paul, is what happens:

"I am afraid of finding quarrels, jealousy, temper, rivalry, slanders, gossiping, arrogance and disorder."

That is the reason why this world is so terrible. The tragedy of the crucified Galilean Carpenter is slight in comparison with the tragedies of the Christs on their crosses from the beginning of time, betrayed, denied, and forced into loneliness and agony by the animal mind. These words are supported by the authority of the apostle whom we have been studying: "The carnal mind is enmity against God." It is the carnal mind in us that is an enemy of the Christ mind in us; and, if we insist on emphasizing our carnal mind, all our prayers to Jesus of Nazareth or to God in heaven are chaff. Until we have found and asserted the Christ in us, our prayers are futile.

The kingdom of heaven lies in our Christ consciousness, and we must reach that consciousness through the struggle to overcome our animal mind. Our animal mind resides in our flesh body. This body exists for the service of our indwelling Christ. We came down out of God from heaven to this earth and took up our residence in this physical body. This body is related to the world order but we have come into the world order to do the Father's business.

We may not yet know why we came into the world, apart from our understanding of what that particular business is, but as we practise it, we discover that we were needed. If we can but touch one life and heal it; if we are but a taper in a window burning through the night for one lost strayed soul, we have fulfilled the business of our incarnation. But we cannot be that taper until the Light of the world is burning in our Christ consciousness.

It is a great difficulty—the difficulty of swinging out of a conventional way of separating Jesus from ourselves, Christ from ourselves, God from ourselves. The result is, we get nowhither. We still practise all the little foolish things that belong to the carnal mind. In spite of our devotions and our agonizing prayers, we cannot climb until we have found that our bodies are temples of the Holy Spirit, the soul, the divine selfhood, our true self.

In the conclusion of his letter to the Galatians St. Paul wrote:

"Brothers, you were called to be free; only do not make your freedom an opening for the flesh, but serve one another in love. For the entire Law is summed up in one word, in *You must love your neighbor as your-self.*"

We have been insisting on trusting our kindness rather than our goodness. If we trust our kindness, our goodness will be manifested; but goodness without kindness is chaff. We shall not enter heaven merely by practising a cold goodness, an ethical obligation to humanity. Unless our hearts are aflame like the heart of Jesus, our goodness is nothing.

So many people have misunderstood the Pauline doctrine of justification by faith. St. Paul meant that anything we do apart from our Christness is of no value. Our goodness is nothing unless it proceeds from our inward dignity, our clearly defined, ascertained and accepted Godhood. The experience which a man has in the practice of his divinity is his justification, and nobody can condemn it except the people in the courts of the consciousness of the flesh mind.

"Take care in case you destroy one another. I mean, lead the life of the Spirit; then you will never satisfy the passions of the flesh. For the passion of the flesh is against the Spirit, and the passion of the Spirit against the flesh."

[296]

If we change the word *passion* to *consciousness*, it becomes clearer. The consciousness of the physical man and the consciousness of the spiritual man are in opposition: "For the passion of the flesh is against the Spirit"—the consciousness of the flesh is against the Spirit. Walk out into the world of the carnally minded and watch them deny the soul. If we begin to change our course of living from that of people still in the outer courts of their consciousness, they will bark and chatter at us. They do not know what it is all about. They are in utter darkness and ignorance. Stand out and begin to bear about in your body the marks of that Christ consciousness. There comes a time in the development of this consciousness when you must no longer consort with unbelievers. There is only one unbeliever—the consciousness that denies the Christ consciousness, the practices of life that overwhelm the practices of the inner life. The most terrible menace against the vitality of that inner life is the practice of those things which St. Paul names:

"Now the deeds of the flesh are quite obvious, such as sexual vice, impurity, sensuality, idolatry and magic."

[297]

Thus he describes the practices of the ancient and of the modern world. Think of loving a woman merely for her body. Think of being married to flesh and bones, and leading flesh and bones up to the altar and being satisfied with that relationship. All the marriage words in the Prayer Book do not sanction that relationship. What happens between men and women under the sway of mere physical consciousness is wrong and condemned. Any relationship, if it be of our physical consciousness merely, or of our dim habits without any consciousness in them, is described by St. Paul as against the soul.

There is a form of idolatry that goes with people of this type. I have seen them—they even go to church. They want holy water. They adore their crucifixes. But it is an idolatrous practice of divine reality. The thing that does not pass from the outer court of our consciousness into our inner consciousness is idolatrous. The use of God, of Jesus, of a sacrament, is idolatrous if it does not awaken our divine consciousness of the resident divinity in ourself.

The magical use of religion is wrong, and

that is why so many people who go to church do not rise. They do not want to be crucified. They do not want to dare the Christ in themselves. They are quite willing to survey the wondrous cross of Jesus on a hill outside Jerusalem, but they are not willing to survey a cross in themselves which must be accepted.

We continue St. Paul's category:

"Quarrels, dissension, jealousy, temper, rivalry, factions, party-spirit, envy, drinking bouts, revelry, and the like: I tell you beforehand as I have told you already, that people who indulge in such practices will never inherit the Realm of God."

And you and I will not, either, if we indulge in those practices. If these things are paramount in our lives, if we are not seeking the inwardness of the kingdom of God, then we shall not find what we mean by life eternal.

Then St. Paul turns to the other list, which we cannot study often enough:

"The harvest of the Spirit is love, joy, peace, good temper, kindliness, generosity, fidelity, gentleness, self-control:—there is no law against those who practise such things. Now those who belong to Christ have crucified the flesh with its emotions and passions."

[299]

Here I would protect myself against being misunderstood. There is nothing wrong in any bodily act. The wrong as such is when the act is divorced from the inward spiritual consciousness. If your soul directs your deed, dare to do it, and let people talk! Be released. "There is therefore now no condemnation to them which are in Christ Jesus, our Lord, who walk not after the flesh but after the Spirit, for the law of the spirit of life in Christ Jesus hath made me free from the law of sin and death." Of course you will be criticized. You will be gossiped about. That will be part of your crucifixion. Men and women of light outer consciousness will be flippant and say all manner of evil things against you. But you must dare to be crucified—your crucifixion may save them. The example of your blameless living, the story of your love and of the graciousness of your ways, will do for them what that same glory and grace in Jesus did for a man like Paul. It started him off on the road to Christhood.

It is here where we honor the name of Jesus. He starts us off. He shows us how. But we must not stand gazing up into heaven. It is not his will. You men of Galilee, why do you stand gazing up into heaven? Why do you seek me there? I am here. I am with you always, even unto the end of the world. Go into all the world and let the light of that indwelling consciousness so shine before men that they may see that God works in you and so come to the consciousness of a God who is waiting to work in them.

II

Paul had a simple, direct, human way of approaching his friends concerning the experience that had changed him from one kind of man to another kind. He was fearless in his dogmatic insistence upon the livingness of that experience. He would make no compromise. He knew that people in Corinth were muttering because of the strange, fearless statements which he had been making concerning the fact of the indwelling Christ, the human soul, son of God; that people were turning bewildered eyes upon one another, asking, "But how can this be true?"

If people say that we lift humanity too high, I answer: You cannot lift humanity any higher than Jesus. We must lift ourselves as high as Jesus, and we must insist on lifting everybody else to the same height. We must take to ourselves, as witness of our worth, the words of him who commanded, "Be ye therefore perfect, even as your Father which is in heaven is perfect." Be satisfied with no standard but that of the highest, of all that you mean by God, and ask for that in yourself. "I have determined to know Christ no more after the flesh." There never was a life so beautifully lived as that life in Galilee and Judea. There never was a love more fully revealed than that love. And yet we must stop going back to Galilee and to Judea. We must stop looking for the sky to open and a miracle to happen that will bring him back. We must look to find him in ourselves.

This was the message that went forth at the Ascension. The disciples had had a wonderful walk with Jesus. He led them to a hill and, when they had reached its summit, he lifted his hands and blessed them, saying, "All power is given unto me in heaven and in earth. Go ye therefore, and teach all nations, baptizing them in the name of the Father, and of the Son, and of the

Holy Ghost: teaching them to observe all things whatsoever I have commanded you: and, lo, I am with you alway, even unto the end of the world."

He who spoke then was a son of God, speaking to sons of God, as I am a son of God speaking to sons of God in terms of Jesus: As my Father has sent me, I am sending you. God sent me in my heart to you. Now God is sending you in your heart to humanity. You have found your Christhood. Go into the world and reveal, by your attitude to people, what you have found, and I shall always be manifested. The power that was in me is now in you. It is the same power—the power of conscious, divine sonship active in people. Rule out everything but your loving kindness. Dare it to the limit, even though you die in the daring. Count this the only sin—that which denies the King of love in you. The only shepherd that you need is your love. That shepherd is your king, and he will guide you.

Wherever this message was preached to men, it startled them. The world had always been divided into two parts, the good and the bad.

Goodness and badness were determined entirely by conformity or non-conformity to traditional standards of conduct. That is why religion to-day languishes, why it is weak. We still insist that people are to be determined by the way they live. We are not to be determined by the way we live. There is no judge but the indwelling Christ consciousness that is ours by inheritance, by nature, and by development. When the Christ in us is fully orbed, we shall discover the Christ in others, however eclipsed, however darkened, however disguised.

So St. Paul wrote: I do not preach to you a little Christ. I am preaching to you the hugest possible Christ conceivable in this universe, the Christ that is incarnated in common human ways. So Elizabeth Barrett Browning understood it when she wrote her famous stanza concerning Euripides:

"Euripides the human, with his droppings of warm tears
And his touchings of things common till they rose to touch the spheres."

It was the Christ in Euripides and in Elizabeth Barrett Browning which met that moment. That which was in Euripides was in Jesus of Nazareth. He did not bring it into the world. It was always here. But how he fulfilled it! How he demonstrated it! How he released it!

The peculiar glory of the Galilean Carpenter is that he took the Christ consciousness as it had never before been taken and lifted it to the height of the Godhood. No wonder, when Thomas came at last into the realization of the Christ in Jesus, he knelt before him and said, "My Lord and my God!" Until I have knelt before the Christ in you and have called it Lord and God, I have not met Jesus. It is the universal Christ. When Tennyson sang in his melodious line,

"Ring in the Christ that is to be,"

he meant this new universal Christ consciousness.

I mark this century as the highest moment in the history of man. Instead of bewailing the lack of humanity, we must acclaim the content of humanity in the possession of its Christ consciousness. Our determination to set people free from the curse of war is the thing that was in

Jesus when he said, "Father, forgive them; for they know not what they do." Let us no longer hate or despise one another. Remember that he who calls his brother a fool, however much he may seem to be a fool, is in danger of dwelling in the hellfire of the outer courts of his human consciousness. It is in the outer court of flesh consciousness that we are hateful and terrible to one another. The only escape is to move from that outer consciousness into the pure indwelling Godhood—our eternal pavilion.

Some of my companions may be troubled by the fact that apparently I rule out God the Father. I do not. How can I be indwelling God unless God who informs all creation should have chosen me as His son, unless He had given me life and consciousness? The point I want to make is, I can only reach the Father through the son, and until I have found myself, I have not met the son. There we have the parable of the prodigal son, with that revealing moment: And when he came to himself, he said, What a fool I am. How many servants of my father have enough to eat and to drink and to wear, while I, his son, am lonely and broken and defeated. There is only one thing for me to do; it is to go back to my father as a son and say I have sinned in disowning my inheritance. I asked for something less, when I had the infinitely more. Forgive me for my folly and at least make me as one of your hired servants.

We cannot get away from God and be happy. The world is throbbing with people who are wretched because they rule out God. Last summer a woman sat on the verandah of a country hotel. A friend opened a little book of poetry and began to read. The other listened attentively, till suddenly she lifted her hand and said, "Close that book. I don't want poetry that refers to God. There is no God." And yet she loved beauty; she loved song. She was like the prodigal son among the swine, eating the husks when by her divine right she should be walking always in the presence of her conscious daughterhood.

We meet these people everywhere. We must do something for them. There is only one conversion. It has nothing to do with conduct, but it has everything to do with discovery. When a man or a woman knows the relation between the indwelling Christ and the eternal all-encompassing Father, sin disappears. We cease to act like swine and begin to behave like sons. When the principle of love directs our consciousness, we do nothing hateful. But our conduct is a mechanical righteousness until we have been purified by the experience of the active indwelling power of our conscious Christhood.

If we seek to be released from the terror, from the peril, from the arrow that flies by day and the pestilence that walks in the noonday, we must dwell in the habitation of the Most High; and the habitation of the Most High is, as St. Paul would say, the Spirit of God bearing witness with the spirit of man that he is His son. When that witness is established, we are no longer under the law of the outer consciousness. We are set free. There is now no condemnation, there is nothing in us that condemns. The Christ does not come into the world to condemn it. Christ does not come into our consciousness to condemn us or to make us wretched or unhappy. He comes into our consciousness to set us free from the law of sin and death.

Our difficulty is in turning our back upon

our idols, our wrong concepts of God that made Him something apart from us, our thinking that the universe could be separated into what is God and what is not God, when God is all in all. "Then cometh the end, when God shall be all in all." The end comes to us when God becomes all of our consciousness, when we no longer think apart from the divine life, when we begin to be to others what Jesus has been to us. We do not have to lead anybody to Jesus. We must be Jesus.

That was the way St. Paul was talking to the Corinthians: I am not offering you a little Christ who died on a cross. I am offering you the resurrected, living Lord Christ, who has taken up his abiding-place in human thought. Go now and manifest him, as he said.

Test your love, however little it may be. Jesus said: If it is as a grain of mustard seed, it will move all your mountains, it will uproot all your forests. Test it against your enemies—against the people who betray and deny and sell you. Test it against the fears and the horrors which possess the people who have not yet moved from the outer into the inner consciousness. It can be done. Jesus did it. St. Paul did it. A multitude have done it. You must be in that company. Move out into humanity under the banner of your Christhood.

VII

THE WAY, THE TRUTH, AND THE LIFE

WE are cowards concerning our heights. When we climb them, we grow dizzy. But if we could only realize that our highest height is but a foothill of still unattained summits, we should not hesitate. Instead of looking down, we should continually be looking up to the summits yet to be gained. So all our soul's adventure would be gay and glad, full of inspiration and power.

The difficulty in the path of our ascent into Christhood is our prevailing indolence and cowardice. Perhaps I should not call them *our*, but they are ours in that we discover them in the outer court of our consciousness. Indolence and cowardice belong to the carnal mind. They are jungle habits. They have nothing to do with the second man, which is the Lord from heaven, that Christ who dwells always in the centre of our selfhood. But because they are so firmly established, it is not easy to pass them.

Christian on his way to Beulah Land had to

[311]

pass by the lions that guarded the gate. They have been severally named by the interpreters of the great mystic Bunyan, but I plead my right to interpret them as indolence and cowardice. I believe that our most insidious enemies are so named, that the reason why we will not allow the Christ in us to be crucified is because we want a little Christ, an easy Christ.

St. Paul knew that. So he assured the Christians in Corinth that when he came to them he was coming with banners flying and with bugles blowing and with swords drawn. It was to be big business, fighting them in the name of this deep, incarnate Christhood. A man, a woman, must gain this Christhood without further avoidance of responsibility, without further compromise.

A friend sent me this excerpt from her private reading, which I use because it is so apt. As we read it, we must ask ourselves this question: Is it not true that the reason why we cannot come over into this glorious discovery is because we are indolent and cowardly?

"How irksome is obedience; the outer you is the spoiled child greedy for new sensation. It runs to

[312]

bright ribbons or gay music down the street. But no
spoiled child grows to man's estate without suffering.
He is disciplined by the antagonisms aroused; discipline and obedience are both a mystery. No one ar-
rives at the holy place [the inner Christhood] undisciplined or disobedient.

"Obedience is irksome for the wild colt and the
stubborn ass—why is discipline necessary? Because
the still, eternal law is in divine order. That which is
ignorant and disobedient perishes. It taketh a thousand to make one. The law is impersonal, inevitable,
and those who obey and cast aside their rebellious
passions are given freedom, protection, and holy
joy.

"In every step from childhood man has been disciplined to meet a standard. What is a standard? An
ideal goal, an ideal man."

The ideal man is our own true self. We must
not make a substitute, not even Jesus of Nazareth. Many of us have been so accustomed to
separating the story of Jesus from our story,
Jesus' sonship from our sonship, that we are
shocked when we are told that the only Christ
that matters is the Christ in us, the son of God
in companionship with the Christ of Jesus, loving Jesus and calling him Master, because our
Christ understands that huge Christ. The little
Christ in us recognizes the giant Jesus. It is
only by such an experience that we can come

[313]

into his presence. It is only by the recognition of ourself as the man we seek that we can walk in harmony with him who said, "Take my yoke upon you and learn of me; for I am meek and lowly of heart; and ye shall find rest unto your souls."

We continue this quotation:

"Man instinctively knows the inner *you*."

For the unseen *you* will always avail.

"What else is good citizenship, good sportsmanship? Men that have been trained since childhood have come to a place where instinctively their inner *you* has stepped to the fore and taken charge. Something deeper than man will always rise up and take charge, for the unseen *you* will always obey. What stood up at Agincourt, Crécy? No spoiled, undisciplined men, but men who from childhood were taught obedience.

"Are you going to be a lazy undisciplined slave to the weaknesses of your outside self? Are you going to let the sleep of forgetfulness steal over your mind and blunt your keen awareness? Are you going to seek soft escape where there is no real rest, nor contentment?"

But we want our soft escapes, we want easy ways. We want opiates and nostrums. We think that by praying to God or by taking a sacrament we have shifted the burden of our cross upon God's back or Jesus' back. Until we shoulder life as a cross and accept its torture and its discipline, we shall not find that rest which remains for the people of God. We must not avoid our life with its problems. We must not avoid society or the people we know. We must not avoid any challenge that comes to us out of the heights of our moment now. If we set our Christ consciousness against those challenges and those problems, we shall be saviours and redeemers.

We have been accustomed to hear man denounced from pulpits as a beast and as a devil. I hope the day will come when the clergy of the Protestant Episcopal Church will remove the note of propitiation from the Prayer Book. I hope the time will come when we shall have the courage to delete from the Communion service such passages as: "Provoking most justly thy wrath and indignation against us."

These doctrines have done more to keep souls from Christ consciousness than all the evil ways of men outside the Church. If we could only have avoided the dreadful fatalism of the pagan

[315]

world which crept into the Bible and the Prayer Book, we today should not be standing where we are, on the verge of a vast crisis that threatens the well-being of civilization. We are where we are because we have denied that inner Christ. The Church is futile because, instead of giving to men the real Christ as it was in Jesus and as it is in mankind, it has given only a pagan conception. Among the people who think that they are most loyal to the spirit of Jesus, who are against this interpretation, are to be found some of the sweetest souls we know— the people who do not want to be disturbed, the people who like to go to church on Sunday and have a pleasant dream, and go out again, feeling that they have done their duty—and that that is all there is to Christianity.

We must dare to become Christs. Dare tradition. How can the people of this commonwealth ever be afraid of the taboo of tradition, when America came into being under the banner of a Christ consciousness that set multitudes free? We must not betray that. Like Peter, we are standing in the court of the high priest denying the Christ of our fathers and of our mothers.

[316]

We must begin to acknowledge that Christ. We must have that Christ in the freedom of our own experience. But we cannot gain the freedom unless we have overcome our indolence and our cowardice.

"When you have found this place you seek, as you have in perception when you have realized it as you can here and now, you will free the imprisoned, lift the darkened into light, open the eyes of the blind that they may see at last how to free themselves, and you will unstop the ears of the deaf who cannot hear the divine whisper."

Is not this a description of a big Christ? Is not this a bigger Christ than the little Christ of tradition, over whom we have quarreled, under whose cross we have shaken the dice of ecclesiastical and theological debate? This real Christ is in you—we are quoting Paul, who, in his letter to the Ephesians, made this statement: I am talking about the real Christ that was in Jesus. I am not talking about Christ Jesus, but I have found a Christ in Jesus, who corresponds to the Christ in me. The difference is that his Christ is grown up, and mine is still a baby. I must exercise my Christhood. I must put it to the test of the experience of a son of God on this planet, against all the things that still find me indolent or cowardly.

In the course of a recent letter from a friend, the statement was made that, in a lecture in a divinity school, a discussion had arisen as to whether Jesus was as important as Eugene Debs. My friend was shocked that such a question could even be brought up. But the question is important. We must find out whether Jesus is as important as Debs; what is there in Debs that would raise that question at all? The questioner was seeing in Debs' courage and sacrifice a resemblance to Jesus. He meant that we have had a man in our century who acted somewhat like Jesus, who brought out this Christ power and made it more real for a boy in this century than it was in the character of a Man who lived two thousand years ago and whose life had been written over so much that the outlines were blurred to him.

I have never been other than an humble disciple of Jesus of Nazareth. All I have by way of the discovery of my own Christhood I owe to that Master. There is only one foundation on which we build this Christ consciousness, the life of Jesus, his manhood, his character, and his infinite love. It is Jesus who gives reality to every beautiful Christ quality that we have since found.

But, on the other hand, I see no reason why anybody should be shocked that in a seminary set apart for training people for the ministry of Jesus a young man of our age, perhaps more familiar with the facts about a certain citizen, should be able to say, "I find in this man what people say was in Jesus." That is not derogatory to Jesus. The Church must have the courage to dare to stand up before this huge young Christ who has never grown old, who is becoming more and more universal, more and more powerful, more and more active in human civilization,—the Christ of our common divinity.

This age can do everything in that name if it will only pass by its lions of indolence and cowardice. If something will only happen in humanity at this moment to resurrect the Christ consciousness, there will be no unrest in Asia, no menace in India, no terror stalking by noon in Russia, no avalanche and devastation of war in China and in Japan, and no uncertainty as to the high destiny of North America. But until we find that, our laws, amendments, and leagues will be powerless against the wave of oblivion that is already lifting its crested head to destroy all that our fathers builded in the name of the everlasting Christ.

If we can accept this, we shall be able to go forth and regenerate society. If we can only dare this huge Christ and come under the discipline of the eternal law, we shall solve our pressing economic problem. "Why will ye die?" asked one of the prophets. . . . Why will you turn aside from the way that is opened unto you? There can be only one answer: We are afraid to go past the lions. We have been so accustomed to think of God sitting on a chair, resting on a sea of glass mingled with fire, with Jesus sitting at His right hand and the Holy Ghost sitting at His left hand, that we are afraid of the notion that the real enthronement of the triune God is in our human consciousness.

We have been baptized in the name of that Father and of that Son and of that Holy Ghost —in the name of that eternal indwelling Father, of that Son which is our self, and of that

Holy Ghost, our self extended in the fellowship of one holy and active experience. We must go past our indolence and our cowardice into the sanctuary of the Most High and be at one with God through the experience of our everlasting sonship.

II

We must put ourselves to the test in our day. We must test ourselves, not our priest, not our church, not even our sacramental systems nor our traditional practices. We must test ourselves to see if we are in the experience—how much of it works in us.

God does not come by the noisy waters of debate, of anger, and of querulous complaining. He comes only when we are silent in some Gethsemane, or are aloof before some worldly Herod, or are alone and lifted above all the world, knowing that we are being crucified, finding our soul in the depth of a darkness that is too utter for description; but always believing in life, always loving it, glad to be taught, eager to be led by the King of love.

If you ask, "How can we find the way into

that silence, into that glimmer of the God-hood?" I repeat, Trust nothing but your kindness. Jesus said: If it is only giving a cup of water, you are on the road to it. Whatever you do in love leads you to it ultimately. You may have to wait. I have heard dear old men and women who have waited through the years of their loving kindness and gentleness, say with Simeon, "Lord, mine eyes have seen thy salvation." Edison lived a life of sacrifice and love. All unconsciously he was demonstrating his Christhood. But it threw no light upon the enigma of himself until suddenly, out of the last darkness of dying and the pause when there were no more words from that great mind, he broke the silence and said, "It is very beautiful over there."

It comes in the fulness of time. We must not be discouraged. We have been warned by the blessed One, the exponent of our Christhood, the Lord Jesus of Nazareth, to keep the light of our kindness burning. However engulfing the darkness of the hatefulness of people, we must be a light in the centre of that darkness. I know of no other way.

THE WAY, THE TRUTH, AND THE LIFE

There came to my desk a few days ago a wonderful poem. When I read it, it seemed to me as though Shelley were alive again; the Sun-Treader had returned to our midst. I am humble before this poem, from the pen of John Hall Wheelock, entitled "Unison," published recently in the *Yale Review*. Here, stated by a young American poet, is the thing we have been seeking to discover:

"There is a secret that the sober mood
  Of science misses, it will not be bought
  By the contriving mind however shrewd—

Within the cell, within the atom sought,
  Within the inner centre's whirling rings,
  Sits the demonic joy that laughs at thought

And is the face behind the mask of things
  And is the measure of the choric dance,
  The music of the song creation sings.

Who shall unweave the web of Circumstance,
  Or trace the pattern in the fugitive
  And shifting tapestry of change and chance?

Or, having learned the pattern, who shall give
  The answer then? What answer has been given
  Ever to any man why man should live!

[323]

Not in the flesh, not in the spirit even,
Not in the cunning of the brain that rides
In mastery upon the roads of heaven,

Or charts the rhythm of the starry tides,
The answer and the truth are found, but where
Deep at the very core the Stranger bides—

And pours his courage through the heart's despair,
And works his healing in the body's wound,
And sheds his glory through the spirit. There

The answer is, the wisdom shall be found,
Which is the answer of the greening tree,
Which is the wisdom of the fruitful ground—

A wisdom older and more wise than we,
Dumb with a secret difficult to tell
And inarticulate with mystery,

For to define it were a miracle."

We cannot put it into words. But we can put
it into a life. Jesus could not put it into words.
In some of his most inspired moments he stammered. St. Paul stammered. The great mystics
all stammer when they come into the realization
of the indwelling God. You remember Newman's
dream of Gerontius? How descriptive Gerontius
is as he climbs to the height, passing all the angels, the thrones and the principalities and

powers; then as he stands in the Presence, all he can say is, "Ah!"

There is no word so vocal as the shudder of the soul when it comes into the presence of its own Godhood. When we have come into that presence, we are set free from all barriers. We no longer seek to know Jesus after the flesh, though, when we find him there, we understand him by the Jesus in our flesh. But our uttermost satisfaction is that we have him now. We are one with him in the life of love, of kindness, of tender devotion to all good causes. By degrees, here a little and there a little, the power grows. It works, as Jesus said, like seed cast into the ground—it comes up day and night, one knows not how. One is conscious only of growth. Somehow, as one goes through life, it becomes more dignified and beautiful, more understanding. One leans less and less on props, and finds in one's self all the strength and all the wisdom. One learns that "of making many books there is no end, and much study is a weariness of the flesh." But the wisdom of God is now in one's own consciousness. It is a light to lighten all the old Gentile thoughts and ways

[325]

and words, filling the world and the universe with light celestial.

> "Oh, not in the low moments but the great
> The exultant rhythm is made audible."

We must eliminate all the low moments. That is what St. Paul did. He said: I forget the low moments. I am no longer in those moods. I remember a time when I was grasping and selfish and hard and mean, when I used to be envious of others, when I was constantly interrupting my Master in myself by an idle curiosity concerning other people's attainments and powers and destinies, saying, with Peter, What shall this man do? and hearing within me the voice of the Master saying, Attend to your own business of Christing. If I will that he tarry till I come unto him, what is that to you to whom I have come, in whom I now dwell? Be guided by that consciousness and by that light alone.

> "Oh, not in the low moments but the great
> The exultant rhythm is made audible
>
> That sways the music at the heart of Fate,
> To which Time in his passage and return
> Moves, and the burdened heavens, with their weight

Of suns and planets, are moving as they burn—
The harmony in which all modes are bent
To the one meaning that they all must learn,

Of many and divergent meanings blent,
Of motions intricate and manifold,
With various voices weaving one consent!

Nor is it easy for the mind to hold
The extreme joy of things, or bear for long
The exalted beauty, hidden from of old,

Whose sure intent, immutable and strong,
Secret and tireless and undeterred,
Moves through the mazes of the winding Song—

And whosoever in his heart has heard
That music, all his life shall toil to say
The passion of it. But there is no word.

They have made no words for it. There is no way."

St. Paul stated it in the Epistle to the Romans, "The whole creation groaneth and travaileth in pain together until now"—waiting for this one consciousness. This consciousness that is in all matter, that is in all experience, becomes at last the very son of God in one's self. In this sense St. Paul was saying good-bye to his friends in Corinth:

"Do you not understand that Christ Jesus is within you? Otherwise you must be failures."

It is important for us to know that. We shall always fail if we think that we can conjure God by a pious act. We cannot. Our whole life is a demonstration of the futility of that way. These things ought we to have done, not to have left the brotherhood of the Christ in us undone and unrecognized. We must find that first. We must first seek God in ourselves, we must seek that rightness in our own inner consciousness, and all these other things will be added unto us.

Of course, we shall use the sacramental system—but with such power! We shall bring a new meaning to people. We shall make an old church become aflame. We shall make society over again, having found that neither this thing nor that thing matters, but this new creation. I assert, in the name of Jesus and of St. Paul, that if we could only be released as they were, we should change all America. Why wait, when the Master of Nazareth is pleading at this hour and saying: Lift up your eyes to the fields. Are they not white and waiting for the harvest?

There's a voice among the voices of the throbbing, restless world,

THE WAY, THE TRUTH, AND THE LIFE

There's a thunder deeper, vaster, than from heaven
    ever hurled,
And you and I have heard it. Listen, still it seems to
    say,
"I have freely given to you. Give, for yours is the
    today."

There's a light upon the mountains and it shines to
    you and me.
There's a mystery, there's a magic, there's a lifting
    ecstasy;
And you and I have seen it in the wonder of the cross,
Let us follow, let us follow, counting selfish gain as
    loss.

There's a shaking of the nations and a rending of the
    veil,
Mountains flowing down like rivers, forests flattened
    by the gale;
For the wind is on our faces and the Spirit is abroad,
Urging you and me to enter the adventure of our God.

Lo, the fields are white to harvest, let us strip to bind
    the grain
Till the fields of golden stubble laugh like flowers
    after rain;
And everywhere one Master is accepted and adored,
In a new earth filled with gladness and the knowledge
    of the Lord.*

When that consciousness comes to humanity,
we shall no longer lean upon the broken reeds
of our old mechanism of the outer consciousness.

* Poem by the author, heretofore unpublished.—Ed.

We shall not seek to acclaim the power of God in this institution, this state, that church, that creed. We shall rely on the Spirit. We shall believe that the Spirit gives life, that the letter kills. We shall look for the holy comradeship of the second-adventing Christ in a new humanity, in a new creation. It will not come to pass until that moment when the followers of Jesus forsake their idols and surrender in obedience to their discovered indwelling Lord.

Would you find the way into that consciousness? Accept the cross on which you must crucify your old vanity. Remember, there will be times when it will hurt and frighten you. There will be times when you will groan in outer anguish: "Oh, that I might escape from the cup of this consequence of accepting my Christhood!" With Jesus you will know all about the cup, all about the denial and the desertion, all about the thorns and the nails, the loneliness and the agony.

There is no other way. Stop pitying yourself. Stop seeking opiates. Your Christ will refuse the drink of vinegar mingled with gall. You will ask no exception. You will not find the way until you have become as stalwart as Jesus. You must set your muscles to the task of your daily living; or, to come back to the answer to the candidate for Confirmation as found in the catechism of our old Prayer Book: "To do my duty in that state of life unto which it shall please God to call me." Is your particular problem physical, mental, or spiritual? Are you lonely, heartbroken, whimpering for somebody to come and help you? Stop. Take it all, and crush it into the cup. Press the grapes until the cup runs over. It is the cup of your Christhood. Lift it up and say, "This is my blood, shed for the whole world. Drink it, all you broken and unhappy and wounded ones. I, too, was broken and unhappy and wounded; and in my Christhood I have found release. Drink it, and go in peace."

We end with St. Paul's concluding salutation to the Corinthians:

"Now, brothers, good-bye. . . . Salute one another with a holy kiss."

Remember that everything we do in love is holy. We must never apologize for our loving

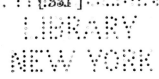

[331]

and our liking. We must dare to be genuine and true. We must listen to the promptings of our hearts. Let people of the outer consciousness bicker about us—they bickered about Jesus. But let us trust our kindness. Let our kiss be holy. Let us meet men and women in the wholesomeness of our Christhood.

May the grace of the Lord Jesus and the love of the eternal Father and the fellowship of the Holy Spirit be in us as we go about the Father's business, binding and releasing, forgiving, healing, helping, making all things new.

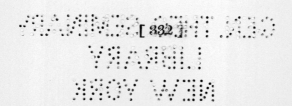